WASHI TAPE CRAFTS

WASHI TAPE CRAFTS

110 WAYS TO DECORATE JUST ABOUT ANYTHING

amy anderson

WORKMAN PUBLISHING
NEW YORK

Library of Congress Cataloging-in-Publication Data is available.
ISBN 978-0-7611-8483-6

Design by Sarah Smith
Photography by Evan Sklar
Additional photography (pages 8–32) by Michael Di Mascio
Prop styling by Sara Abalan
Craft styling by Kirsten Earl

Workman books are available at special discounts when purchased in bulk for premiums and sales promotions as well as for fund-raising or educational use. Special editions or book excerpts can also be created to specification. For details, contact the Special Sales Director at the address below, or send an email to specialmarkets@workman.com.

Workman Publishing Co., Inc.
225 Varick Street
New York, NY 10014-4381
workman.com

WORKMAN is a registered trademark of Workman Publishing Co., Inc.

Printed in China
First printing September 2015

10 9 8 7 6 5 4 3 2 1

CONTENTS

CHAPTER 3: HOME DECOR **71**

CHAPTER 4: JEWELRY AND FASHION **147**

CHAPTER 5: HOLIDAYS AND CELEBRATIONS....**187**

CHAPTER 6: JUST FOR FUN **257**

INTRODUCTION

Maybe it's because my mom was a teacher, but I've always felt a certain responsibility around crafting. Not just to do it and show others the projects I create, but also to teach people how to make them. I truly believe that anyone can be creative; it just takes some practice and commitment (and even a few fails). It's not necessarily something you will be instantly good at.

One thing that helps people learn how to be makers is to start with simple supplies so that they aren't intimidated. And that leads me back to why I started a blog on washi tape. I saw how easy it was to use, how pretty it was, and a lot of potential for many projects. I've always had an affinity for Asian-inspired style and design, so when I saw my first roll of washi tape, the creative wheels started turning. I honestly think I got my first roll of washi tape for free, and when I started the blog *Washi Tape Crafts*, I hadn't even used it that much. But as I did with one of my other craft blogs, *Mod Podge Rocks*, I decided that part of my learning process would occur while I was writing the blog posts. I would try out projects and experiment, and feature others doing the same thing.

When I began my blog, I didn't see that many people using washi tape (outside of other bloggers), but now it's starting to become somewhat of a craft cultural phenomenon. Major retailers sell these fun-patterned tape rolls, and we all just grab them off the shelves with maybe a few ideas of how to use them. And honestly the question I get asked most often is, "I love washi tape, but what can I do with it?"

I really want you to have a great experience with washi tape and this book—I know you're going to love playing, experimenting, and generally being creative. I encourage you to "go crazy" with your tape and not be afraid. Washi tape is truly one of those craft supplies that is "no fail," and there aren't very many that can be said about.

We've included several rolls of washi tape with this book. If you make a project, I'd love for you to share it with me at amy@washitapecrafts.com. I get absolutely thrilled to see what others are making with washi tape, because there really is no end to the possibilities. Now enjoy the book and get washi'ing!

CHAPTER 1

TOOLS AND TECHNIQUES

One of the great appeals of washi tape is that it is so *easy*. It's fairly foolproof. But there are still particular tools and techniques that will all but guarantee crafting success. As with any craft, it's wise to be prepared.

WHAT IS WASHI TAPE?

I get this question a lot, so let's start at the very beginning: Washi tape is a low-tack tape, traditionally made of paper, that's most commonly used in craft projects and design work. In Japan, where it originated circa 2006, it's simply known as "masking tape," but in its short and prosperous life in the United States, it has become known as washi tape (*wa* meaning "Japanese" and *shi* meaning "paper"). Today, many people use *washi tape* as a generic term to describe any patterned tape on a small roll that is tearable and repositionable, even if it's not technically made of paper—but true washi tape is paper-based.

In Japan, washi is commonly made using fibers from the bark of the gampi tree, the mitsumata shrub, or the paper mulberry; it can also be made using bamboo, hemp, rice, and wheat. Though washi tape is made of paper fibers and is easy to tear, it is surprisingly strong—once it's on a craft project, washi tape holds up nicely to wear. I think it's just magical!

HOW TO USE THIS BOOK

I'm excited to share the 110 washi tape projects in this book with you—they represent a variety of styles, types, and looks, ranging from very easy (requiring only a few supplies) to more advanced (requiring a few more supplies—and maybe a little more time). Use this book as an inspirational tool to guide your own washi tape projects. You can complete the project exactly as it's shown, but I encourage you to customize the idea to your needs, to get creative, and—most important—to have fun!

WHY DO I LOVE WASHI TAPE?

Oh, let me count the ways. . . .

- Washi tape comes in an unbelievable number of color and pattern combinations.
- It's very easy to use—you simply pull and tear (or cut) it, and you can start creating!
- Each roll is slightly transparent, so painted or colored paper backgrounds will show through.
- It's temporary and removable; there's no goo left when it's peeled up.
- All sorts of surfaces look good with washi tape, and it has lots of craft applications.
- Washi tape is reusable and biodegradable, and it's made from renewable resources.

HOW TO USE WASHI TAPE

One of the main reasons washi tape is so popular is that it's very easy to use. You simply cut or tear it off the roll and smooth the tape onto the surface of your choice. I really like how the torn edges of washi tape look on some projects. Other times a clean edge makes all the difference. It all depends on the look that you are trying to achieve.

Washi tape is temporary on *most* surfaces and does not leave a sticky residue—but always test if you aren't sure. You'll typically need a sealant to make the look more permanent. Throughout the book, I've included instructions for making washi tape longer lasting if required for a project.

What Will It Stick To?

What I love about washi tape is that it sticks to nearly anything! Washi will adhere to a surface temporarily, and it can be peeled off easily if you decide to remove it—and once it's on a surface, you have the option of making it more permanent with an extra step or two. You can use washi tape on a variety of surfaces, including:

- **Paper and papier-mâché:** *scrapbook paper, cardstock, printer paper, cardboard*
- **Wood:** *picture frames, wooden utensils, doors, pencils, craft sticks*
- **Glass:** *jars, cups, vases*
- **Ceramic:** *mugs, plates, plaques, tiles*

- **Metal:** *kitchen appliances and refrigerators, watering pails, buckets, bicycles*
- **Walls (both painted and not painted)**
- **Cork**

What *Won't* It Stick To?

The following surfaces are difficult (but not impossible) to stick washi tape to. If you see the tape peeling off, you might need a more permanent solution—such as a decoupage medium—to keep the washi tape in place. But that is the wonderful thing about washi tape: If you find yourself in a situation where the tape doesn't stay put, it's that easy to peel it up and start over.

- **Fabric:** *You can use washi tape on fabric for temporary decor (for example, a table runner for a party—see page 93), but, because washi tape isn't washable, you'll need to remove it before you clean your item.*
- **Plastic:** *Washi sticks to plastic, but it might peel back over time. You'll likely need a sealant such as a decoupage medium to keep it down.*
- **Spheres and tapered surfaces:** *Washi tape is straight and flat, so putting it on any surface with a curve, however slight, will cause ruching (the tape will gather, pleat, and stick to itself).*

Sizes and Styles

Washi tape, like most tape, comes in rolls. The most common size available is $5/8$" wide with 25' to 26' of tape. However, as washi tape has become more and more popular, companies have started producing different sizes, so if you look hard enough, you might be able to find widths such as $\frac{1}{4}$", $\frac{3}{4}$", and 3". I've even seen sheets of washi tape!

In terms of colors and patterns, the choices are endless. Just about every time I'm shopping for supplies, I see a pattern I've never seen before. And then I feel that tug: yet another roll I *must* have! My personal philosophy? You can *never* have enough washi tape!

What Can You Make with It?

The answer is: pretty much anything. Despite there being well over 100 projects in this book, it's only the tip of the washi-tape iceberg, because once you feel comfortable with the material, you can mix and match techniques to make hybrid projects, combine techniques, and so on—the possibilities increase exponentially.

What Do You Need for the Projects in This Book?

Obviously, you need washi tape! The rolls of tape that come with this book are meant to jump-start your project making. (Look at the list of retailers on page 301 if you want to get more tape—and you will!) But you'll also need some easy-to-find tools to work with. These are the most common supplies that I use to complete my washi tape projects. I like to have them on hand for any project I'm doing.

- **Washi tape** (*make sure you have the correct sizes and patterns recommended for each project*)
- **Scissors**
- **Ruler**
- **Craft knife**
- **Self-healing cutting mat**
- **Decoupage medium or other similar basic glue or sealant**
- **Pencil**
- **Permanent marker**
- **Cleaning supplies appropriate for the item you're crafting onto:** *paper towels, rubbing alcohol, cotton balls, and so on (washi tape sticks best when the surface is free of fingerprints, dirt, dust, and any other residue)*

You don't need these next supplies for every project, but I use them frequently. They are always in my craft stash and available when I need them.

- **Acrylic paint**
- **Hole and craft punches**
- **Computer, scanner, and printer**
- **Craft glue**
- **Spray adhesive**
- **Hot glue gun**
- **Stencil tape**
- **Floral or beading wire**

BASIC TECHNIQUES

There are several specialized techniques that you can use with washi tape, beyond simply tearing and applying to a surface. Here are some of my favorite techniques—you may find that you'll need to refer to these pages in specific projects. All of them are relatively easy, some may take a bit of practice—but I promise you'll master them in no time.

Tearing or Cutting

Washi can be cut or torn in different ways to create a decorative edge on either the short or long end of the tape. Every time you use washi tape, you'll be cutting or tearing it, so it's important to master the different techniques.

Tearing Rough Edges

It's that simple: Just tear the tape with your fingers. Ripping it gently will create a ragged edge that can make your projects look more rustic and homemade.

Cutting Clean Edges

Use standard craft scissors or a craft knife to create a clean edge with washi tape, whether square, diagonal, pointed, or swallow-tailed. You can also cut washi tape (or sheets of washi tape) to make strips that are smaller in width. Just place a ruler on top (with the piece you want to use visible) and run a craft knife along its edge.

Cutting Complicated Edges

For more complicated decorative purposes, though, place the washi tape onto freezer paper, wax paper, or vellum, and then cut it. The tape peels off these papers easily when you're done.

Cutting Decorative Edges

Use specialty craft scissors to create a variety of edges, from serrated to rounded to lacy and more. As with complicated cuts, place the washi tape on a relatively nonstick surface, like freezer paper, wax paper, or vellum before cutting so that the tape peels up cleanly to restick on your project.

Wrapping

To completely cover a surface with washi tape, you can simply wrap washi tape around the item. Here are a few methods.

SPIRAL WRAP

1 Start the tape at the base of the surface, at a slight angle to the bottom edge. Gently unroll the tape around the surface, maintaining the same angle to the bottom edge.

2 Repeat with a parallel pieces of tape. Trim the edges of the washi tape to fit the surface.

VERTICAL WRAP

1 Tear off one strip of washi tape long enough to cover the surface vertically, then press it down so it's overlapping each edge.

2 Continue adding tape in this way, working your way around the surface until it is completely covered. You may overlap the columns of tape, align the tape alongside the previous piece, or even leave a space in between pieces.

3 Trim the edges of the washi tape to fit the surface.

HORIZONTAL WRAP

1 Start at the base of the surface, and wrap washi tape around the item horizontally until it overlaps itself. Trim the end with scissors.

2 Continue adding tape in this way, until you reach the top. You may overlap the rows of tape, align the tape alongside the previous piece, or even leave a space in between.

3 Trim the tape at the top edge with a craft knife if necessary.

Creating Corners

Any time strips of washi tape intersect, it's an opportunity to introduce a design element. Sometimes you'll want the washi tape to meet in a corner, and, in that case, here are a few different techniques you can use.

MITERED CORNERS

1 Place two pieces of washi tape perpendicular to each other, meeting in a corner. Smooth down.

2 Place a ruler on the 45-degree diagonal where the two pieces of washi intersect and cut, on the diagonal, through both layers of tape. *Note:* Corners need not be right angles to be mitered—any intersection of tape where a clean point is desired is fair game!

3 Use your fingers or tweezers or peel off the excess washi tape. (You'll have to peel back one of the pieces of tape in order to remove a scrap piece, then smooth it down.)

OVERLAPPING CORNERS

1 Place two pieces of washi tape perpendicular to each other, meeting in a corner. Smooth down.

2 Cut along the outside edges of the corner so the tape ends are flush with the edges.

3 Use your fingers or tweezers to peel off the excess washi tape.

ABUTTING CORNERS

1 Place two pieces of washi tape perpendicular to each other, meeting in a corner. Smooth down.

2 Cut along the outside edges of the corner so the tape ends are flush. Then cut along the inside edge of one of the pieces of tape so the adjacent tape end is flush with the inside edge.

3 Use your fingers or tweezers to peel off the excess washi tape.

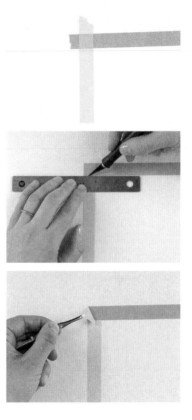

CROSSED (OR OXFORD FRAME) CORNERS

1 Place two pieces of washi tape perpendicular to each other, overlapping in the corner and extending a distance beyond the intersection. Smooth down.

2 Measure, mark, and cut the tape extensions so that they are the same length. Cut them at a 90-degree angle, or on the diagonal. *Optional:* Leave the torn edges uncut for a more relaxed look.

3 Use your fingers or tweezers to peel off the excess washi tape.

ADVANCED TECHNIQUES

Washi tape is so accessible as a material that even the advanced techniques are pretty easy to tackle, once you're comfortable with the basics.

Making Patterns

One of my favorite things about using washi tape is combining different patterns. With the right color combinations, you can use two, three, or even up to five patterns on a single project. It helps to include a few solid colors with the patterns so the project doesn't look too crazy—but the great thing about making something yourself is that those decisions are all up to you.

LAYERING

Don't throw away those washi scraps—instead, think creatively and repurpose them into a collage. You can layer and overlap different colors and patterns onto a piece of paper, and, if you like, cut out shapes from the layered paper. If you cut out shapes, simply glue or decoupage them onto another object.

WEAVING

There's some math involved in this technique. You have to take into consideration the surface of the project, as well as the width of each of the tapes you're using, in order to evenly space the tape. Before you start your project, practice layering the tapes that you plan to use so you can see how they'll look when woven.

1️⃣ Measure the surface you plan to cover and cut several lengths of washi tape to fit. For example, if you are working on a 12" × 12" surface, cut strips at least 14" long (a little excess never hurts!).

2️⃣ Determine how wide the warp and weft (vertical and horizontal lines, respectively, in traditional weaving) will be and mark them on your surface.

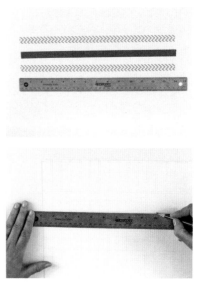

❸ Start the weaving on two adjacent sides of the surface. Apply two strips, allowing the tape to meet at a right angle. Press the warp strip down first, then smooth the weft strip over it, leaving the rest of both strips loose (in fact, press a strip of wax paper onto the underside to keep it from getting tangled) until you apply more strips.

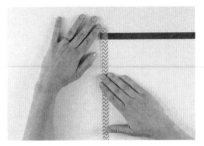

❹ Add another strip on either side of the two applied in Step 3. This time, press the weft strip down first, then smooth the warp strip over it. Continue adding strips, two at a time, in this manner, until you reach the second set of marks from Step 2.

❺ When the pattern is complete, run a hand over the surface one more time to make sure all areas are smoothed down.

Making 2-D Shapes

Once you've mastered pattern-making, apply another step to your process! It can be very satisfying to make shapes out of washi tape—either freehand or with punches—and you can use them to decorate almost anything.

FREEHAND OR PATTERN CUTTING

For freehand cutting, use a craft knife and self-healing cutting mat. A sharp blade allows for smooth and intricate cuts.

1 First, make a template: Select the shape or pattern you want to use, size it appropriately on the computer (scanning it first if necessary), and then print.

2 Place a piece of wax paper (vellum and freezer paper also work) over the shape, and cover it completely using washi tape, making sure to overlap the tape approximately ⅛".

3 Remove the shape from underneath the wax paper and put it on top of the overlapping washi tape. Secure the layers with stencil tape. Use the craft knife to cut around the shape, making sure to go through all the layers (the paper, washi tape, and wax paper).

4 Separate the layers and use tweezers to peel the large washi tape sticker from the wax paper.

5 Then place the sticker on any surface you like!

Note: *On a smaller scale, this technique also works with paper punches. Stick the washi tape to the wax paper and slide both layers into the punch. See more on page 22.*

PUNCHING

Aside from making washi tape stickers using a craft punch, you can also transform plain paper or cardstock into decorative scrapbooking paper just by adding washi tape. Any craft punch will work with washi tape, as long as it's very sharp.

1 Press strips of washi (overlapping the pieces of tape or not) onto vellum or cardstock, and punch out shapes using various craft punches.

2 Use these pieces to embellish any project.

Making 3-D Shapes

Washi tape is great for two-dimensional designs, but it's perfect for three-dimensional shapes as well. Use the following techniques to make unique shapes that will add a pretty flourish to any project.

SIMPLE PETAL FLOWER

1 Cut a 5" to 6" piece of thin floral or beading wire and bend it into a petal shape, twisting the ends at the bottom.

2 Fold washi tape over both sides of the wire petal and press the tape together. Trim around the washi tape with scissors to create a petal shape. Repeat until you have the desired number of petals.

3 Twist the bases of all of the petals together at the bottom, wrap the stems in floral tape, and then spread out the petals to create a flower shape.

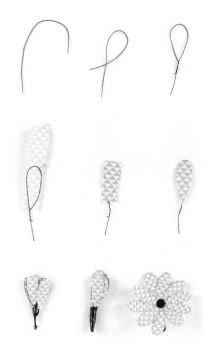

WRAPPED FLOWER

① Use a craft punch to punch a circle out of cardstock. Draw a spiral shape on the circle and cut along the line.

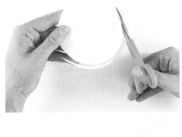

Note: *In order to create a petal effect (see Charmed Bracelet, page 163) without the use of a specialized machine, cut a scalloped edge along the outside edge of the spiral to the center.*

② Cut or tear the washi tape into thin strips. Wrap the washi tape around and around the spiral shape, perpendicular to the cut edge, the entire length of the piece of cardstock.

③ Coil the taped cardstock spiral tightly around itself. Secure the washi tape at the bottom of the coil with tacky glue or a hot glue gun.

BENT PETAL FLOWER

1. Cut two 2" pieces of washi tape, then press them together, adhesive sides in.

2. Fold the piece in half so that the short ends meet. Then fold again lengthwise.

3. Cut an arc along the open end to give the petal a rounded edge.

4. Unfold to reveal a lozenge shape. Then fold each long edge into the center.

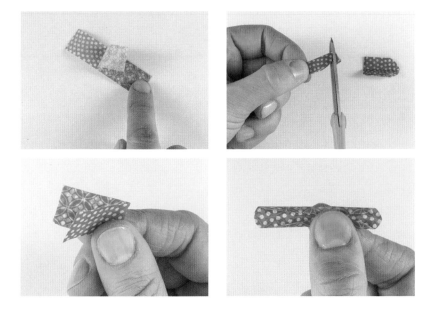

5 Fold in half, to make an accordion fold.

6 Fold the petal in half, pinching the fold to crease. Repeat Steps 1 through 5 to make two additional petals.

7 Arrange all of the petals together, folded points in. Then use a hot glue gun to adhere them to each other.

8 Add an embellishment to the center of the flower with hot glue to help secure the petals.

ROSETTE

① Cut a 12" × 1" strip of cardstock and press a length of washi tape along one long edge. Then accordion-fold the cardstock, making folds about every ¼".

② Glue the ends of the paper together to form a cylinder, making sure the paper isn't twisted.

③ Press down the top edge of the cylinder into the center to make a circle.

④ Then secure with hot glue to a piece of paper or wooden circle. *Optional:* Add an embellishment centered on top to finish.

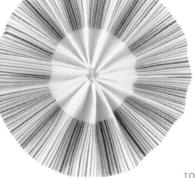

BOW

1 Cut a length of washi tape that is approximately twice as long as you'd like the resulting bow to be. For example, if you'd like a 5" bow, cut a 10" strip of washi tape. Cut a second piece of washi tape that is about 1" to 2" longer than the strip in Step 1. Fold each piece of washi tape onto itself, sticky sides together. Make sure the edges line up, then press and smooth carefully.

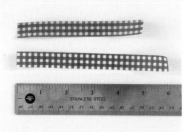

2 Join the two ends of the longer piece of tape with a small piece of washi tape to create a loop.

3 Pinch the loop in the middle (against the seam) to make a bow. Keeping it pinched, center the bow on the piece of washi tape from Step 1.

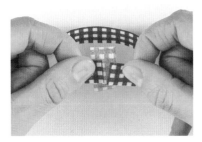

④ Wrap an additional length of washi tape around the bow loop and the shorter piece of washi tape.

⑤ Cut a small triangle from each end to create V shapes that complete the ends of the bow. Then apply to a gift!

EMBELLISHING AND FINISHING

Printing, Writing, and Stamping

You can print, write, or stamp on your washi tape to further embellish it. Before you start, test any ink you plan to use to make sure that it won't smudge or rub right off the tape.

PRINTING

1 Open a word-processing program and type the text you'd like to see printed on the tape. Size the text according to the size of the washi tape, leaving a healthy margin around the word or phrase. Print the text on printer paper.

2 Press strips of washi tape over the text on the paper so they'll be placed correctly to catch the ink the second time the paper is fed through the printer. Smooth the tape thoroughly, then feed the same sheet of paper (*with* the washi tape on it) back through the printer.

③ Give the ink a few minutes to set, then spray with a clear matte acrylic spray to prevent the ink from smudging.

④ Once dry, peel up the printed tape from the paper and place it on your project.

WRITING

As long as it passes the smudge test, any Sharpie or permanent marker should work to write on washi. Use it to create a label or to write a message to paste on a card.

STAMPING

Washi tape also looks great when rubber stamped. For example, if you want to create a card, weave a background out of washi tape (see pages 18–19) and stamp a message right on top of it. Before you stamp, test the ink, letting it dry completely, to make sure that it won't smear.

Decorating

Add rhinestones, buttons, sequins, embellishments, and more to your washi tape with tacky glue. Let dry according to the instructions on the bottle.

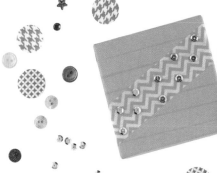

Weatherproofing

Washi tape isn't waterproof, so if you want your creation to stand up to all sorts of weather, add a layer of sealant. You can technically use washi tape on items for outdoor use, but be careful about leaving tape in direct sunlight. Most washi tape fades if exposed to regular, strong sunlight. You'll also want to test any weatherproofing products on the washi tape before committing, so you can make sure there isn't a reaction that might alter the color, texture, or adhesiive quality.

CHAPTER 2

GOODS AND GIFTS

DRESSED-UP NOTEBOOKS

If you're going to take notes, why not have a fashionable spot to write them? Rather than spend too much on designer notebooks, buy the plain-Jane budget versions and decorate them yourself—with exactly the patterns and colors you want. *Note:* This totally works on sketchbooks, too!

SUPPLIES:

A plain notebook

Spray adhesive

White label paper the same size as (or larger than) the notebook

Craft knife and self-healing cutting mat

Ruler

Pencil

Washi tape

Note: *If the notebook is already white, proceed directly to Step 4.*

1 Coat the front cover of the notebook with spray adhesive, then smooth down the white label paper over it.

2 Flip the notebook, then fold the paper around the binding. Add more spray adhesive, avoiding the binding so that the notebook can bend freely. Smooth down the paper.

3 Place the notebook open on the cutting mat. With the craft knife, trim the label paper all the way around the edges of the cover.

4 Close the notebook, then measure and mark a horizontal line halfway up from the bottom edge. Press a strip of washi tape along the mark, wrapping it around to the back side, and leaving a little tape hanging over each edge of the notebook.

5 Repeat, adding horizontal strips evenly spaced below the first until the bottom half of the cover (front and back) is covered.

6 Wrap the tape ends around the edges of the cover and secure them to the inside of the notebook. Trim as necessary. (You can leave a little bit of the washi tape edges for interest or trim them away completely.)

7 With the same or different color washi tape, press a strip that extends vertically from and perpendicular to the top horizontal stripe, letting the end extend off the top edge of the cover.

8 Repeat, adding evenly spaced vertical strips parallel to the first strip along the front and back cover.

9 Wrap the tape ends around the edges of the cover and secure them to the inside of the notebook. Trim as necessary.

TRY THIS NEXT:
Apply the washi tape in an exclusively vertical or horizontal pattern—or diagonally!

FRIENDLY PHOTO COASTERS

Coasters are a perfect addition to pretty much any home decor, and custom coasters with washi tape and photos make an excellent gift. Just remember to seal them well, especially if the gift recipient (or you!) loves drinking really hot beverages.

SUPPLIES:

4 to 6 ceramic tiles, 4" x 4"

Computer with a photo-editing app

Digital photos of pets or children

Color laser printer and laser print paper
(so the colors won't bleed
while decoupaging)

Scissors

Paintbrush

Decoupage medium

Washi tape

Pour-on high-gloss finish

Craft knife and self-healing cutting mat

Adhesive cork shelf liner

Note: *If you don't have access to a color laser printer, you may also use an inkjet printer. Let the ink dry for 5 to 10 minutes, then lightly coat with a matte spray acrylic sealant on both sides. The sealant will protect the ink from smearing when you apply another medium over it.*

1 Use a photo-editing app to size your images to fit on top of the ceramic tiles with a $\frac{1}{2}$"–$\frac{3}{4}$" margin on all sides. Print the photos on laser print paper, then trim to the size of your coasters.

2 Paint decoupage medium onto the back of one photo, center it onto the surface of a coaster, then

smooth it down with your hands to secure it in place. Repeat with the other coasters. Let dry for 15 to 20 minutes.

3 Use strips of washi tape to create borders around the photos, overlapping the photos as desired.

4 Paint another coat of decoupage medium on top. Let dry.

5 Protect the coasters from heat and moisture with the high-gloss finish. Raise each coaster off of your work surface with a small, stable, but disposable item like an inverted yogurt container.

6 Follow the manufacturer's instructions to mix the finish, then pour it in the center of each coaster, coaxing it to the edges, so that it covers and drips over the sides and corners.

7 Let dry without moving or handling for at least 24 hours.

8 Cut any remaining drips off the bottom edge of the coaster with a craft knife.

9 Press the bottom of each coaster onto the adhesive side of the cork shelf liner, and use the craft knife to trim the excess cork around the edges.

PERSONALIZED COFFEE TUMBLER

Who doesn't want a personalized to-go cup? This one's a great gift for the big-time coffee drinker in your life—even if the big-time coffee drinker in your life is you. Washi tape is a far more colorful way to customize your tumbler than, say, the faux name scribbled by the barista at your local Starbucks.

SUPPLIES:

Coffee tumbler with removable insert

Scissors

Washi tape

1 Remove the inside chamber from the tumbler and then remove the paper insert that comes with it.

2 Starting at one edge, press strips of washi tape over the paper insert. Cover the entire sheet with tape, letting the tape ends extend over the edges of the paper.

3 Trim around the edge of the insert to remove the excess washi tape.

4 Slide the insert into the tumbler and reinsert the inside chamber.

Note: *Remove the washi tape insert before washing the mug. Reinsert when it is dry.*

TRY THIS NEXT:
Use paper punches to cut out shapes and apply them to the insert for another layer of decoration.

CUSTOM CLIPBOARD

Nothing makes me happier (or more inspired) than seeing a good old to-do list clipped to one of these embellished boards. Sometimes the motivation to cross things off is all in the presentation!

SUPPLIES:

Clipboard with removable clip

Screwdriver

Paintbrushes

Acrylic paint, in white

Ruler

Pencil

Washi tape

Tweezers

Craft knife and self-healing cutting mat

Decoupage medium (optional)

1 Use a screwdriver to take out the screws holding the clip in place. Remove the clip from the clipboard and set aside all hardware.

2 Paint the entire clipboard with acrylic paint. Layer on two to three coats and let dry.

3 Measure approximately $1\frac{1}{2}$" down from the top of the clipboard on either side and mark with a pencil.

4 Run three strips of washi tape across the top from left to right, overlapping them slightly and lining up the patterns on the tape.

5 Place two strips of a different color washi tape right below the three strips applied in Step 4.

6 Repeat Step 5 below, using a third tape color.

7 Repeat Steps 5 and 6, alternating colors, until the entire clipboard is covered.

8 Use the ruler as a straight edge, and gently score the tape along 1" diagonals in both directions.

9 Use the tweezers to peel up the tape as desired to reveal the white paint below in triangular shapes.

10 Flip the clipboard over and trim the excess washi tape from around the edge with the craft knife. *Optional*: Paint decoupage medium over the surface in order to secure the tape and make it more durable.

11 Use the screwdriver to reattach the clip.

PET SILHOUETTE ART

Like many dogs and their people, my dogs are like family to me. But it can be hard to get them to sit for a portrait! In this project, you'll take your (or a friend's) pet's sweet silhouette and turn it into handsome wall decor, customized with your favorite washi tape colors and patterns.

SUPPLIES:

Digital photo of your pet in profile

Scissors

12" × 12" sheet of plain scrapbook paper

8" × 10" frame, preferably with an oval mat

Computer with a photo-editing app and printer

Printer paper

Washi tape, in a similar palette

Clear contact paper

Stencil tape

Craft knife and self-healing cutting mat

1 Use scissors to trim the sheet of scrapbook paper to fit the 8" × 10" frame, then set it aside.

2 Use a photo-editing app to size the photo of your pet in profile (facing either left or right) so the head is about 4" across. Print it.

3 Align strips of washi tape onto the contact paper to create a shape larger than the size of the pet profile.

Note: *You can run the design vertically, horizontally, or diagonally.*

4 Align the photo of your pet over the washi-taped contact paper. Use stencil tape to hold down the layers

on the cutting mat. Use the craft knife to trace the outline of the pet's silhouette. Make sure to cut through all layers.

5 Remove the stencil tape, locate the washi-taped contact paper cutout underneath, and peel off the backing from the contact paper.

6 Center the silhouette onto the trimmed scrapbook paper, then press and smooth to adhere it. Place the photo mat on top, and insert your creation into the frame!

TRY THIS NEXT:
Use any silhouette—even inanimate objects such as cars, flowers, or buildings. A child's toy would make a sweet silhouette in a nursery!

5-MINUTE GARDEN MARKERS

Practical and decorative, garden markers given the washi tape treatment add a dash of flair to any planter. This project allows you to label everything in your green space, and you can assemble the markers in minutes.

SUPPLIES:

6" wooden plant markers

Washi tape

Scissors

Permanent marker

Clear outdoor spray sealant

1 Laying the plant markers flat, cover one side with a strip of washi tape and then cover the other side.

2 Trim the excess tape with scissors if necessary.

3 Use a permanent marker to write the name of the plant at the top of both sides of the garden marker.

4 Spray the outdoor sealant on one side of the garden markers. Let

them dry. Then flip them over and spray the other side.

5 Let the markers dry 24 hours before sticking them in soil.

TRY THIS NEXT:
Make outdoor sealant your new friend. As you expand your outdoor washi tape repertoire, try decorating your garden tools, watering can, and planters!

DRESS 'EM UP CLOTHING HANGERS

I've long since graduated from college, but recently I looked into my wardrobe and wondered why I still had the same plastic hangers common in dorm rooms. Time for a change! These wooden hangers are a great way to achieve killer closet style, whether you're still living it up at college or firmly in the grown-up world. They also make great gifts, especially when presenting handmade clothing items.

SUPPLIES:

Wooden hangers

Painter's tape

Spray primer, in white

Washi tape

Craft knife

Decoupage medium, in satin finish

Paintbrush

1 Mask any portion of the hangers that you don't want painted (like the metal hooks) using painter's tape.

2 Spray primer onto the hangers in a well-ventilated area. Spray one side, let it dry, and then spray the other. Check to see that the hangers are fully coated, and repeat as necessary.

3 Starting at the top of your hanger, right under the metal hook, run the washi tape horizontally from one side of the hanger to the other (you can tear off at the ends, leaving a little excess).

4 Repeat directly underneath that piece of washi tape. Instead of overlapping, match up the pattern with the piece above it. Repeat until the entire hanger is covered on one side.

5 Use your craft knife to trim the washi tape. Do so right along the edge of the hanger, very lightly, so you don't scratch the spray paint.

6 Trim carefully around the ends of the hangers, since the washi tape strips are small in those areas and can peel up or tear easily.

7 Repeat on the other side of the hanger.

8 Paint a layer of decoupage medium over the tape to seal it.

TRY THIS NEXT:
Make a set of matching hangers to give as a present on the occasion of a child getting her own bedroom.

WRAPPED PAPIER-MÂCHÉ LETTERS

One tried-and-true method for quick room, home, or party decor is to decorate papier-mâché letters. Depending on the size, they can take up a lot of space, but the personalization opportunities are endless: initials at a wedding reception for the DIY bride and groom, your kids' initials on the door or wall of their room, or as table decoration (if you cover the front and back) at a birthday party for your favorite pal. If the letters are small, you could even spell out a whole name or short inspirational quotation!

SUPPLIES:

Papier-mâché letter(s)

Washi tape

Craft knife and self-healing cutting mat

Paintbrush

Decoupage medium

1 Stick a strip of washi tape horizontally across the top front of the selected letter. Stick a second strip directly below the first, lining up the strips as closely as possible. Continue placing strips in alternating colors, ignoring any holes in the letters (like P, D, or B) until the front is completely covered.

2 Flip the letter, tape side down, onto your cutting mat, and use your craft knife to cut around the inside

and outside edges of the letter, trimming off the excess tape (the letter should be visible again!).

3 To cover the sides of the letter, start on the inside or the bottom (where a seam won't be visible) and wrap a strip of washi tape around the outside, parallel to the edge of the letter.

4 Continue taping the inner and outer edges, overlapping tape as necessary. Use a craft knife to trim any edges as needed.

5 Repeat Steps 1 through 4 on as many letters as you choose.

6 Paint two coats of decoupage medium on each letter. Let it dry.

TRY THIS NEXT:
Attach your letters to coat hooks near the front door, so everyone has a personalized spot to hang up his or her coat at the end of a long day.

TO DO

- ☑ WAKE UP
- ☐ DRINK COFFEE
- ☐ WALK the DOG
- ☐ BAKE COOKIES

ABSOLUTELY MAGNETIC

Magnets are popular because they are incredibly easy to make and are perfect for gifts. Beginning crafters love them, and kids can even join in on the action.

SUPPLIES:

Flat glass marbles

White cardstock

Pencil

Scissors

Washi tape

Silicone sealant

Toothpick

Hot glue gun

Magnets with a smaller diameter than the marbles

① Set the flat glass marbles on the white cardstock and trace them. Use the scissors to cut out the shapes.

② Cover the shapes with strips of washi tape. Trim around the edges of the shapes with scissors.

③ Spread silicone sealant onto the washi-taped shapes with a toothpick, and then press the flat side of the marbles on top. The silicone sealant will spread; wipe any that seeps out the sides. Let dry.

④ Hot-glue the magnets to the back of the marbles. Let dry. Then scatter them on your fridge or metal file cabinet.

TRY THIS NEXT:
Place a small photo or a sticker in the center, over the washi tape, to personalize each magnet for the gift recipient.

SIMPLE STRIPED FRAME

Using washi to decorate picture frames definitely captures the essence of this Japanese tape: cute and easy. If you are a beginning washi enthusiast, this frame is a great place to start. Once you make one, you'll want to tape up the whole house. Promise!

SUPPLIES:

Unfinished wooden frame with removable backer

Paintbrushes

Acrylic paint, in white

Washi tape, in coordinating colors and varying widths

Craft knife and self-healing cutting mat

Decoupage medium, in matte finish

1 Apply several coats of paint to the frame, then let it dry.

2 With the frame faceup on your work surface, press one strip of washi tape diagonally across the frame, approximately in the middle.

3 Apply the next two strips of washi tape directly above and below the first. Continue to add strips, working from the center of the frame outward.

4 When the frame is covered, place it facedown on the cutting mat, and use the craft knife to trim the excess tape along the inside and outside edges of the frame.

5 Paint the entire frame with a few coats of decoupage medium to seal it. Then let it dry before inserting a photo.

QUICK-AND-EASY GIFT TAGS

On the days when your supply of cards and labels is running low, or you need to tag a party favor at the last minute, you'll be grateful for this quick project. Because they require so little setup, these tags are easy to make one at a time as needed—or, make dozens the next time you have 30 minutes to yourself, so you have a stash on hand that can be personalized with the name or message of your choice each time there's a gift to be given!

SUPPLIES:

White blank gift tags, 1⅜" × 2⅛"

Washi tape

Craft knife and self-healing cutting mat

Pen

Baker's twine

1 Remove the white strings that come with the gift tags.

2 Press strips of washi tape onto the cutting mat, and cut them lengthwise into halves (to make narrower strips). Carefully peel them up in order to apply them to the gift tags.

3 Wrap the thin washi tape strips at alternating angles around each tag, leaving a ¾" to 1" space clear to write a greeting.

4 Write the gift recipient's name or a greeting (Happy Birthday!, Congratulations! I think you're swell!) in the space between the strips.

5 Thread the baker's twine through the top hole in each tag and tie the ends in a knot.

OUT-OF-THE-BOX GIFT WRAP

If you have a roll of washi tape handy, there's no need for wrapping paper or ribbon—just use brown or white paper as your base and get your decorating on with any pattern you like.

SUPPLIES:

Kraft or other plain paper

Clear tape

Scissors

Washi tape

1 Unroll or flatten the kraft paper, and center your gift on top. Wrap it as you would normally, using clear tape to secure on the bottom and at the sides.

2 Press strips of washi tape in evenly spaced stripes, from one end to the other, around the entire width of the package, using one pattern of washi tape.

3 Repeat on the longer side of the package with a different tape pattern.

4 Make sure your washi tape meets on the bottom of the package, and smooth the ends together thoroughly.

TRY THIS NEXT:

- Cut the tape into 1" strips and create evenly spaced crosses or Xs across the package.
- Weave two washi patterns into a square, then cut a shape from it.
- Use washi tape to draw a picture on the top of the package of a traditionally dimensional embellishment like a flower or a bow.

EASY-TO-EMBELLISH ENVELOPES

Here's a simple method to dress up that random collection of excess envelopes you've accumulated over the years. The next time you write a letter, stick it in one of these refreshed envelopes, and you'll make your pen pal's day!

SUPPLIES:

Plain envelope(s)

Washi tape

Scissors

1 Orient the envelope with the address side facing up.

2 Starting at the left side of the envelope, press a strip of washi tape all the way across the bottom edge, letting half of the washi tape extend off the bottom.

3 Fold over the washi tape to the back and smooth down.

4 Trim the excess tape at each end.

5 Repeat Steps 2 through 4 down each side of the envelope and across the top.

6 Pull the envelope flap open and do the same along its edge, but instead of folding over the excess (you don't want to cover the adhesive on the envelope), use scissors to carefully trim it off.

7 Trim and smooth any remaining edges. Now slip a note inside and send it!

TRY THIS NEXT:
Is it time to send out a batch of seasonal cards? Just grab a holiday-themed roll of washi tape for your envelopes!

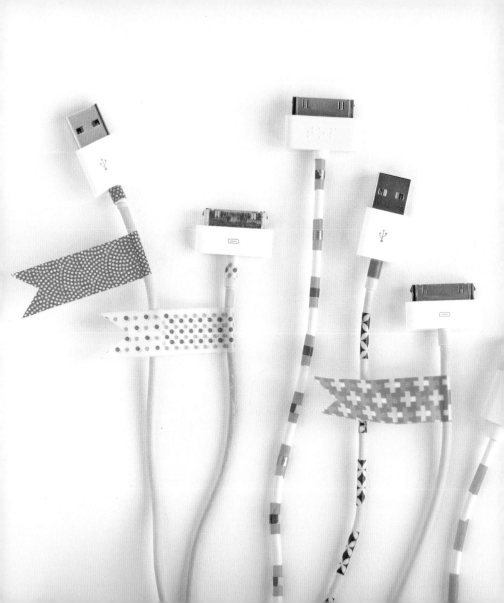

CORD ORGANIZATION SYSTEM

It's nearly impossible, in any modern household, not to amass an overwhelming collection of chargers and cords for our electronic devices. And finding the right one (or distinguishing yours from someone else's) in the tangle of cables can be like finding a needle in a haystack. But with a simple labeling system you can keep your cool—and have cool-looking cords to boot.

SUPPLIES:

Electronic cords and chargers

Washi tape

Ruler

Scissors

Permanent marker or pen

1 There are multiple ways to label your cords and chargers. Here's one way:

a. Tear a 6" piece of washi tape from a roll and wrap it around the electronic cord about 2" from its end. When you get to the end of the washi tape, fold it on top of itself, creating a little flag, and smooth.

b. Use scissors to cut a triangle into the end of the washi tape, turning it into a pennant.

c. Write a name or other identifier onto the washi tape using a permanent marker or pen.

2 To distinguish a cord without a label, simply wrap washi tape around the cable every 1". Start at the top, wrap and trim, then repeat, all the way to the bottom.

PRICELESS PHOTO MAT

On a recent trip to the craft store, my friend educated me on the importance of photo mats. "You can't use just white," he said. "There are so many other colorful options!" He was right, but the price wasn't. With washi tape, however, I can have the best of both worlds: a splash of color and savings.

SUPPLIES:

Frame with a photo mat

Washi tape, in 4 colors/patterns

Ruler

Craft knife and self-healing cutting mat

1 Remove the photo mat from the frame and place it faceup on your work surface.

2 Select your washi tape patterns (1, 2, 3, and 4) and review the diagram on page 70. Starting at the left edge of the mat and going all the way to the right, place a strip of Tape 1 horizontally about 1" above and below the mat window.

3 Starting at the top edge of the mat and going all the way to the bottom, place two lengths of Tape 2 vertically on the mat, about $1\frac{1}{4}$" to the left and right of the mat window. Place a piece of Tape 2 vertically about $1\frac{1}{2}$" outside each of the two previous strips of Tape 2 .

4 Place a strip of Tape 2 about 1" above the top strip of Tape 1, and a strip of Tape 2 the same distance below the lower strip of Tape 1.

5 Center a strip of Tape 3 between each pair of vertical strips of Tape 2.

6 Press two lengths of Tape 4 onto the cutting mat. Use the craft knife to cut a $\frac{1}{2}$" zigzag pattern down each

length. One at a time, carefully peel up each strip half and press the halves about ¼" above and below the horizontal Tape 2 strips.

7 Smooth down all the washi tape. Wrap the ends of the tape around to the back of the frame, or trim the edges with the craft knife. Insert the photo mat back into the frame. Stick in your favorite photo and display!

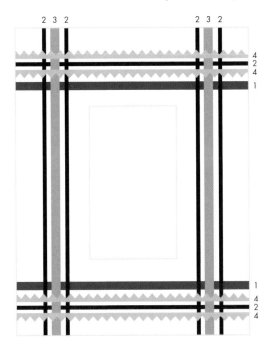

CHAPTER 3

HOME DECOR

STATEMENT CEILING FAN

You can spend quite a bit of money on a stylish ceiling fan, but here's a way to revamp a plain one to fit your decor—without breaking the budget. This project is especially nice for a nursery that'll eventually need to transition into a kid's room: Just peel off the tape when you need to change up the theme.

SUPPLIES:

Ceiling fan

Washi tape, in 2 coordinating colors or patterns

Tape measure or ruler

Pencil

Scissors

Craft glue (optional)

1 If your ceiling fan is straight out of the box, skip to Step 2. If it's already installed, grab a step stool (and, if possible, a helper) and clean the blades thoroughly. Make sure the fan is turned off.

2 Measure and lightly mark every 2" along the length of each blade.

Starting close to the base, wrap a length of washi tape along the first pencil mark until the two ends meet. Stick the washi tape to itself to secure.

3 Add a strip in another color at the second pencil mark. Continue adding strips every 2", working from the center of the ceiling fan outward.

4 If necessary, use a dab of glue to keep the washi tape seams together on top of the fan blades.

5 Repeat Steps 2 through 4 on the remaining fan blades.

GNOMENCLATURE BOOKENDS

This whimsical set of bookends invites the outdoors in by adding a touch of the forest to your home decor. Use your favorite miniature items to customize the top of the bookends with the woodland scene of your choice.

SUPPLIES:

Sand or aquarium gravel

Zip-top bags

2 sturdy cardboard gift boxes, about 8" × 5" × 5"

Hot glue gun or adhesive dots

Washi tape, in wood-grain pattern and an accompanying bright color

Scissors

Paintbrush

Decoupage medium

Gnome, toadstools, or other woodland-themed plastic figurines

1 Pour about 1 cup of sand or aquarium gravel into two zip-top bags, seal them, and then insert a bag into each gift box. Apply glue to the lids and close them. Let them dry.

2 Apply the washi tape vertically to the four sides of the boxes, lining up the tape to create a continuous wood-grain pattern. Wrap the tape edges over the top, and trim the tape ends about ¼" from the edge.

3 Press strips of the second washi tape color over the top of the box, trimming again at the edges.

4 Use a paintbrush to coat the boxes with decoupage medium to seal the washi tape. Let them dry.

5 Apply glue to the bottoms of the plastic figurines and arrange them on the top of the boxes. Let dry completely before placing on a bookshelf.

SHIPSHAPE WALL ART

Do your children have a particular theme or shape that they're obsessed with? Of course they do. You can turn that obsession into fun wall art for their room with washi tape. This can be done with any silhouette or cutout of their choosing. The creative direction is up to you, er, them!

SUPPLIES:

2 sheets of cardstock, in white and one other color

Ruler

Pencil

Scissors

Washi tape, in 10 –12 colors or patterns

Glue stick

Frame, with mat included

1 Use the ruler and pencil to draw a geometric (or other) shape onto one sheet of cardstock. Cut it out.

2 Lay strips of washi tape horizontally over the shape.

3 Continue placing tape until the shape is completely covered. Then trim around the edges to remove the excess tape.

4 Arrange the washi-taped shape over the second sheet of cardstock, and use the glue stick to secure it.

5 Place the design inside the frame and hang your newest art piece.

PAPER PLANES WALL MURAL

The drawback to vinyl wall murals is the risk of tearing off paint (or worse, drywall) when the vinyl stickers (eventually) come down. Enter washi tape, stage left. With washi, you can throw up a mural, take it down, change it up—all without worrying about wall damage. I adore these paper planes—but you can pick any object you want to adorn your wall!

SUPPLIES:

Wall space

Pencil (optional)

Ruler (optional)

Washi tape, in two colors

Scissors

1 Lightly sketch the outline of a paper airplane on the wall with a pencil and ruler. (Alternatively, because the tape is repositionable, you can freehand the design and avoid marking up your wall altogether!)

2 Press washi tape over each of the lines, trimming the corners as needed so the intersections come to a point.

3 Snip triangular pieces of tape about $1/2$" long and arrange them behind each airplane, about $1^{1}/2$" apart, as dashed movement lines. Now step back and admire!

CROSS-STITCH CANVAS

Cross-stitch has become very popular in home decor, and—surprise!—you can achieve the look with washi tape, too. I love the look of cross-stitch, especially when it's interpreted using materials other than traditional embroidery floss. You can even follow actual cross-stitch patterns to create your projects—simply enlarge the pattern to fit the canvas, and then "stitch" away!

SUPPLIES:

24" × 48" canvas

Paintbrushes

Acrylic paint, in white or a color of your choice

Cross-stitch pattern diagram

Computer, scanner, and printer

Stencil tape

Transfer paper

Pencil

Washi tape, 7mm width, in different shades (9 are used in the rose, shown)

Ruler

Scissors

Decoupage medium

1 Start by painting the canvas with 1 or 2 coats. Let it dry completely.

2 Scan the cross-stitch pattern diagram, enlarge it approximately 800% to fit your canvas, and print it (on several sheets of paper, if necessary, tiling them together with tape).

3 Use stencil tape to affix the enlarged cross-stitch pattern to your canvas, with the transfer paper sandwiched in between.

4 Use the pencil to trace the pattern, which will transfer the

design onto the canvas. *Note:* If your transfer paper is small, move it around underneath the pattern as you work.

5 Peel off the pattern and transfer paper to reveal the cross-stitch design transferred to the canvas.

6 Cut several 1" pieces of washi tape and place them onto the canvas, using the original pattern for color reference.

7 To keep the "stitches" consistent, place all the left-leaning tape pieces first, followed by all the right-leaning pieces, to complete the crosses. Repeat until the design is complete.

8 Use decoupage medium to coat the canvas and seal the washi tape. Let it dry completely before hanging.

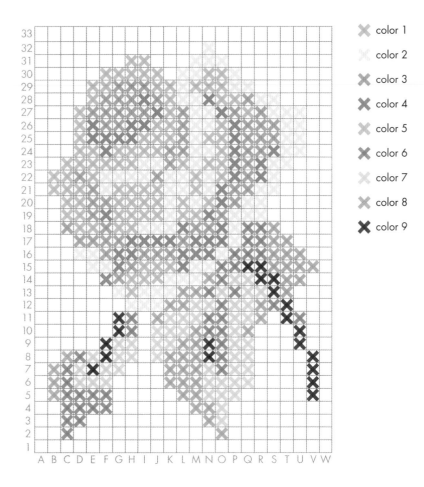

color 1
color 2
color 3
color 4
color 5
color 6
color 7
color 8
color 9

SWITCH PLATE UPDATE

Sometimes you need a quick and easy way to update a room—and sometimes you find that way with washi tape! Covering switch plates is simple and fun—and especially great for kids' rooms, craft studios, or man caves.

SUPPLIES:

Light switch plate

Screwdriver

Cotton ball

Rubbing alcohol

Craft knife and self-healing cutting mat

Washi tape, in 2 or more patterns

Scissors

Foam brush

Decoupage medium, satin finish

1 If you have a new switch plate skip to Step 2. Otherwise, turn off the power and unscrew the screws above and below the light switch to remove the switch plate from the wall. Clean it with a cotton ball and rubbing alcohol.

2 Place the switch plate right side up on the cutting mat. Starting at one end, lay a strip of washi tape horizontally across the switch plate. Press a second strip of tape next to the first. Continue to line up strips of washi tape (with or without space in between them) until the switch plate is covered.

3 Flip the plate over and use scissors to trim the tape around the edges, leaving a $\frac{1}{4}$" margin. Then fold the excess tape over the edges of the switch plate. At the corners, cut out a V shape to create a dart before folding to keep the tape from bunching up.

④ With the plate still upside down, use the craft knife to cut an X through the rectangular hole. Fold the triangular flaps of excess tape around the edges of the rectangular opening.

⑤ Use the tip of the craft knife to poke through the tape at the screw holes. Insert and remove the screws to cajole the excess tape through the holes.

⑥ To protect the tape and make it easier to wipe off grimy fingerprints, use the foam brush to apply a light coat of decoupage medium in the direction of the tape. Allow it to dry completely before installing (or reinstalling) the plate over the light switch.

TRY THIS NEXT:
Coordinating all of the switch plates, including outlet covers, in a room is a fun touch.

WOODEN WASHI TRAY

Trays are incredibly useful items in almost every room, whether they're helping serve up breakfast in bed, holding small trinkets on a coffee table, or organizing items in the bathroom. Use this method of arranging washi tape to customize a tray for your home. Bonus: Trays are one of the most readily available craft surfaces ever—you can find them at craft stores, mass retailers, even thrift shops.

SUPPLIES:

Unfinished wooden tray

Paintbrushes

Acrylic paint, in two colors that coordinate with your washi tape

Ruler

Pencil

Washi tape, in 2 colors

Craft knife

Spray acrylic sealant

1 Coat the entire tray with acrylic paint. Let it dry.

2 Use the ruler and pencil to lightly mark the center of the tray, then arrange 4 strips of tape in a diamond shape around the center point. Cut 4 more strips of tape in a different color, and arrange them around the first diamond, creating a second diamond. Repeat a third time with slightly longer pieces of tape, in a different color, to create another, larger diamond. Cut the ends of the tape strips so the vertices of the diamonds meet cleanly.

3 Add diamonds on either side of the central diamond with washi. Trim with a craft knife where the tape overlaps.

④ Arrange a strip of washi tape so it extends from each of the outer diamonds to each side of the tray. Cut the ends so they're even with the sides of the tray.

⑤ Spray a layer of acrylic over the surface of the tray to seal the tape. Let it dry completely, 24 to 48 hours, before using.

⑥ To clean the tray surface, wipe it with a damp paper towel.

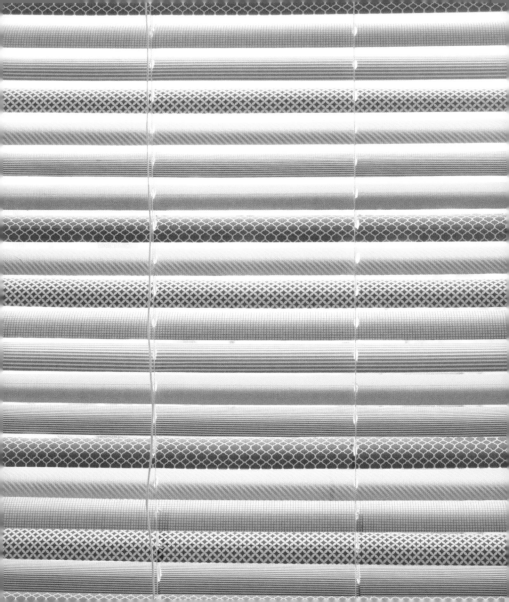

WISHY-WASHI WINDOW BLINDS

Several years ago I lived in an apartment where painting the walls wasn't allowed, and the landlord wouldn't stand for having any holes in them, either. Needless to say, this severely limited my ability to decorate! Here's a way to add some much-needed color to a room without worrying about causing any damage. Simply peel off the tape when you move out, and everyone gets their security deposit back!

SUPPLIES:

Plastic or metal window blinds

Tape measure

Washi tape, in 6–8 coordinating colors

Scissors

1 Measure the width of the window blinds in three segments: the distance from the left edge to the cord, the distance between the cords, and the distance between the cord and the right edge (which should match the left side). *Note:* Some blinds have more than two cords running down the blinds; you'll need to measure each segment separately.

2 Cut strips of washi tape to match the measurements of the blinds. Then stick the tape strips onto the convex side of each window blind segment (one color per segment), smoothing as you go. Allow the excess to hang over the edges.

3 Trim the excess tape with scissors.

4 Repeat Steps 2 and 3 with each slat until the blinds are covered.

TUMBLING GEMS TABLE RUNNER

When I was growing up, my mom always placed a runner down the center of our kitchen table. It made our plain wood table look pretty, and it's a tradition that I've carried into my own home. The nice thing about this particular runner is that the designs are temporary—simply peel up the washi when the next holiday or celebration comes along and replace it with a new design.

SUPPLIES:

Clear tape

Scissors

Wax paper

Washi tape

Ruler

Pencil

Table runner, in a smooth, lint-free fabric

1 Cut 2 strips of clear tape, about 5" long.

2 Place the strips of clear tape on a sheet of wax paper, parallel to each other and about 5" apart.

3 Lay strips of washi tape from one clear tape strip to the next, filling in the space between them completely. The strips of washi tape should just barely overlap.

4 Use the ruler and pencil to mark 5- and 6-sided polygons.

5 Trim the tape around the pencil lines, and peel the edge of the shapes from the wax paper.

6 Position the shapes onto the runner as desired.

CLOTHESPIN WREATH

Clothespin wreaths have been adorning doors for decades. There's a reason for their staying power: ease and versatility. I made one for my mom several years ago, and she still has it hanging in her home—it's one of her favorite handmade gifts from me. In this washi tape version, the size, colors, and patterns are all up to you, and there's no need to tailor this wreath to a particular season. Bonus: It won't ever fade or shed its needles!

SUPPLIES:

MDF wreath form

Spray paint, in a complementary color to your washi tape

Clothespins, about 65 (enough to go around the perimeter of the wreath form)

Washi tape

Scissors

Paintbrush

Decoupage medium

Hot glue gun

Floral wire

12" ribbon

1 Spray-paint the wreath form one side at a time, and let it dry. Line up the clothespins around the wreath form, like spokes on a wheel, to determine exactly how many clips to cover with washi tape.

2 Working one clothespin at a time, press a length of washi tape onto the top of the clothespin and trim off the excess tape around the edges. Repeat on the remaining clothespins. If you're using more than one color/pattern of washi tape, note the number of

clothespins you'll need in each color to complete your pattern.

3 Paint a layer of decoupage medium over of the washi-taped clothespin surfaces to seal them. Let dry.

4 Hot-glue the clothespins, decorated side out, around the wreath form. Let them set.

5 Wrap a length of wire around the MDF wreath and twist the ends together to make a loop. Thread a ribbon through the wire loop to hang the wreath.

TRY THIS NEXT:
Select washi tapes from your stash that are all different shades of the same hue and arrange them over the clothespins to create an ombré effect.

FAUX WALLPAPER

Sometimes you just want an easy way to change up a wall: to herald a new season, as a backdrop for an impromptu photo booth, or to set the scene for a party. This washi tape wallpaper is that easy way you've been looking for.

SUPPLIES:

Small span of wall space

Tape measure

Pencil

Ruler

Washi tape (approximately 4 rolls will cover a 12" × 12" square of wall)

Scissors

Craft knife

1 Measure the height and width of the wall, and press your pencil tip to make a dot at the midpoint.

2 Working left and right from this point, mark a pencil dot every 12".

3 Measure and mark a row of dots 12" below and 12" above the first row.

4 Continue making rows 12" above and 12" below the previous rows until the entire wall is marked.

5 Find the dot in the lower left corner. Measure 6" up from that dot, then measure 6" to the right, and mark another dot.

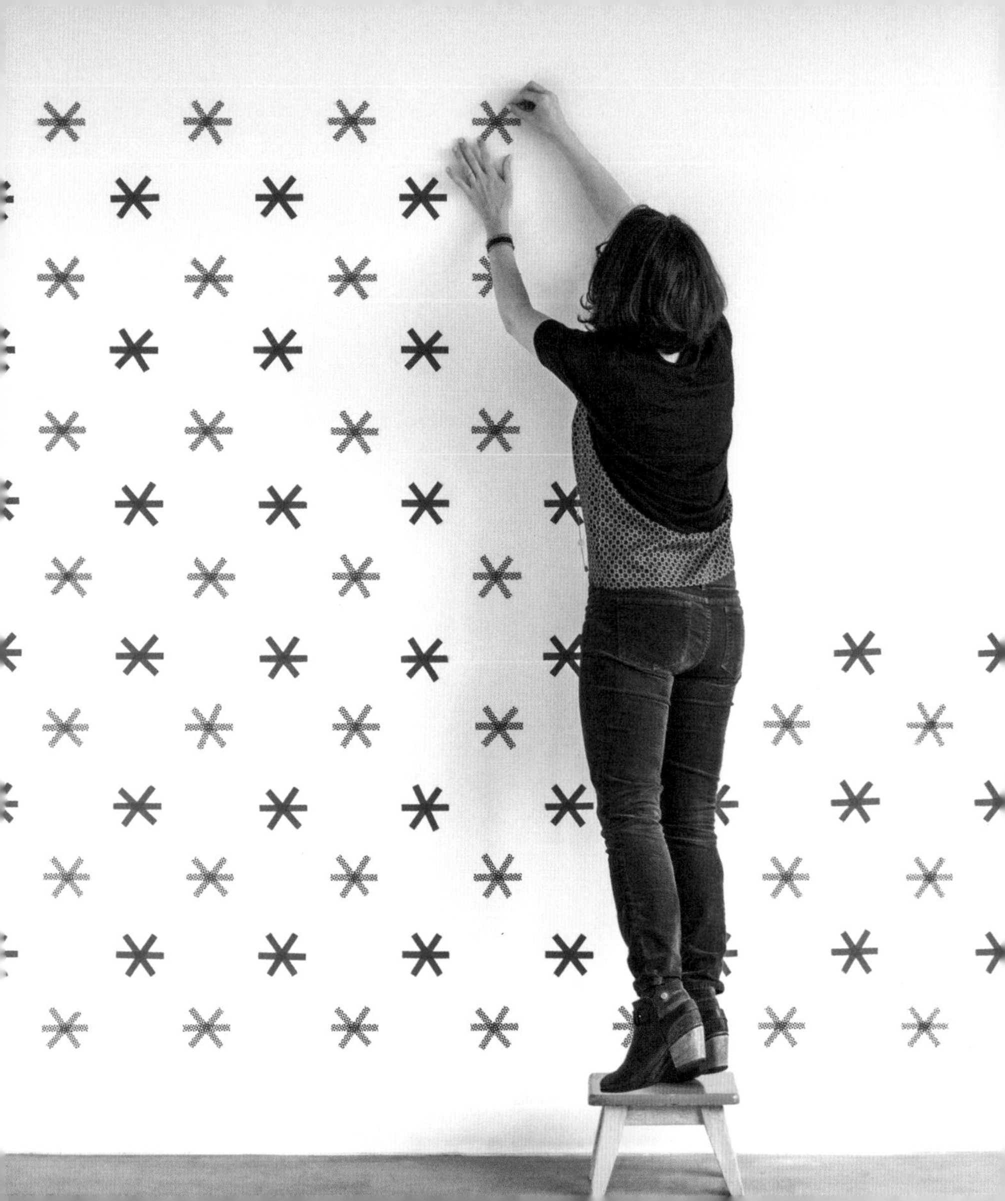

6 Moving to the right, measure and mark dots every 12" from the dot marked in Step 5.

7 Repeat Steps 5 and 6, starting at the second dot up from the bottom, then the third, and so on, on the left side, until there is a full set of dots 6" from the original set (the rows of dots should appear staggered, like a brick pattern).

8 Cut the washi tape into 4" strips.

9 Using three strips per asterisk, place one strip horizontally and cross the other two in an X, centering the intersection of the three strips over the pencil dot.

10 Repeat Steps 8 and 9 until the entire wall space is covered.

TRY THIS NEXT:
Create a repeating pattern of any shape that you like: hashtags, plus signs, or dashes and dots for a hidden Morse code message.

DREAMY HEADBOARD

This is the perfect project for the temporary home (a first apartment or a dorm room)—you save money by not purchasing a headboard, and when your lease is up, you just peel it up and go!

SUPPLIES:

Wall space at least as wide as your mattress

Tape measure

Pencil

Washi tape, 1 roll in 2" width and 2 rolls in ⅝" width

Craft knife

Level (optional)

1 Start by figuring out how large the headboard needs to be. The bottom of the headboard should start at the top of the mattress or slightly below and should measure 32" in height. To determine the width, keep in mind that typical headboards are about 3" wider than the mattress on either side (or add 6" total to the standard mattress measurements: twin 38", full 54", queen 60", king 72").

2 Use the tape measure and pencil to mark the dimensions of a rectangle on the wall—no need to draw the complete rectangle, just make pencil marks for the corners.

3 Run a length of washi tape from the bottom left to the top left to define the left edge of the rectangle, and repeat on the right side.

4 With another length of wide washi tape, connect the two sides of the rectangle, checking that the tape strip remains parallel to the floor. (*Optional:* Use a level as a guide.)

Trim the ends of the tape at the corners so that they don't overlap.

Note: *The measurements in Steps 5–9 are based on those of a standard twin bed. Make adjustments as needed for larger beds.*

5 Starting from the inside edge of the top left side of headboard, mark along the inside top edges at 2", 4", 6", 8", 10", 12", 14", 16", 18", and at 22", 24", 26", 28", 30". Mark along the inside bottom edge at 16", 18", 20", 22", 36", and 38".

6 Press a strip of thin washi tape so that it runs diagonally between the 2" mark at the top and the 16" mark at the bottom. Then press a strip connecting the 4" mark with the 18" mark. Add two more parallel diagonal strips, moving right across the rectangle.

7 Measure down the right edge of the fourth diagonal strip, and make marks at 2", 4", 6", 8", and 10".

8 Press a strip of thin washi tape (in another color) so that it runs diagonally between the 2" mark on the diagonal and the 10" mark along the top edge. Then press a strip connecting the 4" mark on the diagonal with the 12" mark at the top. Add three more parallel diagonal strips, continuing to move across the rectangle.

9 Press a strip of thin washi tape (in the first color) so that it runs diagonally between the 22" mark at the top and the 36" mark at the bottom. Then press a strip connecting the 24" mark with the 38" mark. Add three more parallel diagonal strips, moving right across the rectangle. *Note:* The bottom edge of these last three strips of tape will intersect the right edge.

10 Trim all the overlapping edges with the craft knife so the tape intersections are neat.

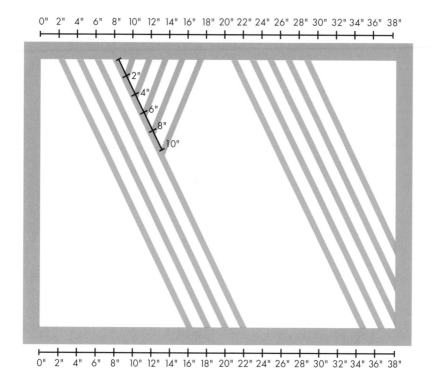

SOFA STEM REFRESH

This may be the quickest washi tape transformation of them all—and, for that reason, it's extremely satisfying. Add a subtle punch of color to your living room in minutes just; adapt the instructions to match the length of your couch legs.

SUPPLIES:

Sofa with legs

Washi tape in 2 to 4 colors

Ruler

Glue (optional)

Scissors

Decorative-edged scissors (optional)

1 Wrap one strip of washi tape around a sofa leg, about 2" to 4" up from the bottom, making sure to overlap the tape at the back of the leg so that the tape is secure. *Note:* If the washi tape isn't sticking well to itself, add a dab of glue to help secure it.

2 Wrap a second strip of washi tape about ¾" above the first. The two rings will appear as horizontal stripes. *Optional:* Use decorative-edged scissors to cut the top or bottom edge of each strip.

3 Add a third stripe to the couch leg, if desired, then repeat the pattern from the first leg on the remaining three.

TRY THIS NEXT:
This project concept also applies to entertainment center legs, table legs, and more!

DRY-ERASE LABELS

Although getting organized can be utterly satisfying, coming to the conclusion that you have to reorganize can feel downright exasperating. Allow me to let you in on two secrets: bins and dry-erase labels. Bins will hold all types and sizes of supplies, while dry-erase labels offer a practical, modifiable solution to classifying your clutter, in case you decide to move things around. Made from dollar-store frames and decorated with washi tape, the labels can be written on (bin contents or person's name), then easily erased and edited when necessary.

SUPPLIES:

Frames with a clear glass or plastic insert (from the dollar store or dollar bins at your local craft store)

White cardstock (optional)

Pliers

Washi tape

Scissors

Adhesive Velcro

Canvas storage bins

Dry-erase markers

1 Remove the backs of the frames, including the paper insert (if there is one).

Note: *If the frame doesn't come with a paper insert, measure and cut one from white cardstock.*

2 Use pliers to carefully (and permanently) remove the frame stand—you won't need it.

3 Press strips of washi tape onto the paper insert to completely cover it (work either vertically,

horizontally, or on the diagonal). Trim the excess tape around the edges with scissors.

4 Return the washi-taped insert to the frame and secure it (make sure that the clear plastic or glass is still in place!).

5 Stick a piece of the hook part (rough) of adhesive Velcro to the back of the frame, and stick the corresponding loop piece (soft) to the center of the front of one of the canvas bins.

6 Repeat for as many frames and storage bins as you have.

7 Attach the framed labels to their respective bins. Now you can use a dry-erase marker to write on the clear surface and switch the labels around as needed!

TRY THIS NEXT:
Don't limit yourself to labeling bins. Try labeling shoe cubbies or coat hooks or lockers so every member of the family always knows where to find her or his footwear.

FAUX FLOOR RUG

I love the concrete floor in my craft studio—all of the paint splatters and glitter give it such character. But there's another (less messy!) way to give a hard floor surface character, and it starts with washi tape. The best part of a washi-style floor rug is that it doesn't cost hundreds of dollars.

SUPPLIES:

Concrete (or other uncoated) floor

Measuring tape

Pencil

Washi tape, in a variety of colors (the example shown here features 31 different tapes in varying widths, ⅛" to 2")

Craft knife

Decoupage medium (optional)

Paintbrush (optional)

1 Measure a 2' × 3' rectangle on the floor. Use the pencil to mark the corners.

2 Grab an entire roll of washi tape (a light or white shade is best) and start unrolling it, from one corner to the next adjacent corner, creating one side of the rectangle. Press it to the floor.

3 Continue around the rectangle, laying down the remaining three sides. Overlap the tape where the strips intersect.

4 Once the rectangular frame is in place, use the remaining rolls of washi tape to create a pattern over the framework that was laid in Steps 2 and 3. For a basic striped pattern,

alternate adding a strip of washi tape at each 2' end of the rectangle, moving toward the center. *Optional:* Mark additional shapes or patterns, like diamonds, zigzags, chevrons, a geometric pattern, or a more free-form design, over the stripes.

5 To create flat fringe, press a 2"-wide strip along each of the 2' ends of the rug. Use the craft knife to cut out slivers of tape 1" to $1\frac{1}{2}$" into the edge. *Note:* Cutting right on the floor is easiest on a cement floor. For wood floors, or other softer surfaces, press the piece of tape onto wax paper and cut the fringe on a cutting mat before peeling back the wax paper and transferring the fringed tape to the floor. *Optional:* Depending on the foot traffic you expect your faux floor rug to sustain, you may choose to coat the surface with decoupage medium to slow regular wear and tear.

Note: *This project is best done on a concrete floor or other uncoated surface, since washi tape doesn't stick very well to vinyl or laminate without a sealant.*

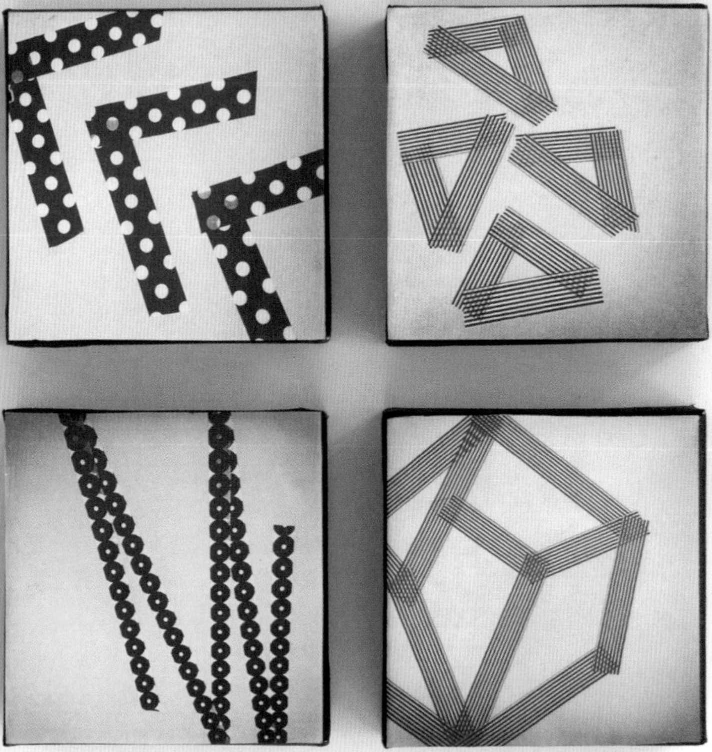

INSTA-WALL ART

Honestly, I would be happy just sitting and looking at my collection of washi tape. It's so pretty! But to take that notion a step further, here's a way to turn a love of washi collecting into canvas art—so instead of just decorating the inside of a drawer or bin, it's decorating a wall (and giving you a more reasonable excuse for staring at your washi tape!).

SUPPLIES:

Four 4" × 4" gallery canvases

Paintbrush

Acrylic paint

Washi tape

Paper (optional)

Smartphone with Instagram app (or other photo app that provides filters)

Computer with a photo-editing app

Laserjet printer and printer paper (at least 32 lb.)

Scissors or craft knife and self-healing mat

Spray adhesive

1 Brush acrylic paint onto each of the four canvases, then let them dry.

2 Press washi tape, in any design, onto a flat surface or paper.

3 Take four square-framed smartphone pictures of the washi tape designs and apply filters using Instagram or any other photo app. *Note:* The images can be four different photos or one photo filtered four different ways.

4 Upload the four images to your computer and size them to 4" × 4", then print them.

⑤ Cut out each image with scissors or a craft knife.

⑥ Working one at a time, use spray adhesive to attach the photos to the front of a canvas.

⑦ Smooth thoroughly, and let the adhesive dry. *Optional:* Use strips of the washi tape you photographed to decorate the sides of the canvas.

⑧ Hang the quartet in a row, column, or a 2 × 2 grid, and admire your masterpieces!

TRY THIS NEXT:
Split one picture across multiple canvasses and hang them in such a way that they tile together to complete the image.

UPCYCLED DESK ORGANIZER

To start this classic project, just raid the recycling bin for a few bean or tomato cans. Inspired by a desk organizer I made years ago from recycled cardboard rolls and a cereal box, I decided to create a new, updated version, drawing inspiration from a different recycling bin. It adds the perfect fun touch to a desk set, and you can customize to add as many compartments as needed.

SUPPLIES:

Cans, clean and empty, in 28-, 14-, and 6-ounce sizes

Paintbrushes

Acrylic paint, in white and a color to match your washi tape

Wooden plaque

Pencil

Washi tape

Craft knife and self-healing cutting mat

Scissors

Decoupage medium

Hot glue gun

1 Apply white paint to the cans and the matching color to the plaque. Give each several coats to ensure opacity, then let dry.

2 Arrange the cans on the plaque, clustering them together, and mark their locations with a pencil.

3 Select one can and wrap a strip of washi tape around its top and base, overlapping the ends about $1/4$" at the back. *Optional:* Press a strip of washi tape just inside the top of the can to conceal any rough edges.

4 Repeat with the remaining cans.

5 Apply additional strips of tape parallel to and between the two strips, at varying distances. *Optional:* Cut the standard-width tape into narrower strips for visual variation.

6 Paint a coat of decoupage medium over the washi-taped cans to seal the tape in place. Let dry for 20 minutes and then paint on a second coat for extra durability. Let dry once more.

7 Squeeze glue around the bottom edge of one of the cans and glue it onto its mark on the plaque. Repeat with each can until all cans are glued in place. Let the plaque dry for 24 hours before using.

SWEET SPICE JARS

Smart-looking spice jars inspire me to cook more—mostly because they make me want to spend more time in the kitchen, gazing at the adorable containers holding cinnamon sticks, nutmeg, and cloves. In a neat, well-organized kitchen, who knows what could happen next . . . pumpkin soup?

SUPPLIES:

Clear spice jars

Washi tape, in standard and narrow widths, in complementary colors

Label maker with clear labels

Scissors

1 Press a standard strip of washi tape around each of the spice jars, about 1" from the lip of the jar. Trim the ends so they overlap about ⅛" to ¼".

2 Add a narrow strip of washi tape in a coordinating pattern about ⅛" on either side of the first strip. Trim the ends.

3 Use the label maker to print out the name of each spice onto clear strips. Center each label over the wider washi tape strip and smooth it down.

TRY THIS NEXT:
These little jars can help you organize your craft room, too! Use washi tape to sort and label your beads, sequins, or other knickknacks.

PHOTO-TRANSFER PILLOW

Because washi tape is paper-based, it doesn't hold up so well in the rain or on flexible surfaces . . . until now! By using iron-on transfer paper, you can permanently transfer any design your heart desires onto a fabric surface! I love this idea for pillows and any other home decor textures you can imagine.

SUPPLIES:

White cotton pillow, preferably with a removable outer cover

Washi tape, in bright, bold patterns

Printer paper

Scanner, computer with a photo-editing program, and inkjet printer

Iron-on inkjet transfer paper

Scissors

Iron

1 Press several strips of washi tape onto a sheet of printer paper in a design you like for your pillow.

2 Place the design facedown onto the scanner bed and scan it. Use a photo-editing program to make any tweaks as desired.

3 Print the image onto iron-on transfer paper and cut it out.

4 Place the transfer paper sheets facedown onto the pillow cover.

5 Press each section, one at a time, with a warm iron. Do not remove the paper backing until all sections are ironed on and have cooled.

6 Once cooled, peel back the transfer paper to reveal the image on the fabric. Put the cover back on the pillow.

CHEERY CHAIR UPGRADE

Chairs can go out of style, but that doesn't mean you want to spend the money to replace them. This project takes a basic chair from traditional to modern with the addition of some paint and washi tape. It's simple, it's stylish, and you won't believe how easy it is.

SUPPLIES:

Chair, with back spindles

Paintbrush

Acrylic paint, in white

Pencil

Washi tape, in 3 complementary colors

Scissors or craft knife

Foam brush

Decoupage medium

Sandpaper (optional)

Primer (optional)

1 Paint the chair white, then let it dry. *Note:* If you're refurbishing an existing chair, you'll need to first sand the chair to remove any existing paint, then prime it.

2 Use the pencil to lightly sketch a rhombus shape (an off-kilter diamond) across the back spindles of the chair.

3 Select one color of washi tape and press a strip vertically along one of the spindles, extending from the top down to the first sketched line of the rhombus. Add 1 to 2 more strips, as needed, to completely wrap the top of the spindle. Repeat on the other spindles.

④ Select a second color and wrap it around the bottom portion of the spindles, extending from the bottom up to the sketched line.

⑤ Use the scissors or craft knife to cleanly cut the edges on the sketched diagonals.

⑥ Wrap the third washi color around the chair legs, starting from the bottom and extending up at varying intervals. Use the scissors or craft knife to cut the top edge of each of the taped sections on an angle.

⑦ Using a foam brush, coat the taped sections with decoupage medium to keep them from peeling. Let dry.

TRY THIS NEXT:
There are so many directions you can go when revamping a chair. Cover the spindles in alternating colors, or across the the color specturm in a rainbow, or cover only the seat in washi tape.

WOVEN-TOP END TABLE

An end table offers a smooth, even surface for showcasing one of my favorite washi tape techniques: weaving. Once you get the hang of it and find your rhythm, the technique is easy—and the results are stunning.

SUPPLIES:

Small, square end table

Tape measure

Pencil

Washi tape, in 3 colors

Craft knife

Brush-on clear sealant

Paintbrush

1 Use the tape measure and pencil to mark the center point on each of the four sides of the table top.

2 Measure and make a mark 1" on either side of the four dots. Repeat, making a mark 2" on either side of the same dots. Repeat one more time, making a mark 3" on either side. You should have 7 marks 1" apart on each edge of the table surface.

3 Starting on one edge of the table top, press a strip of washi tape from the center mark to the center line on the opposite edge. Use the craft knife to trim the tape at each edge.

4 Rotate the table one quarter turn and repeat Step 3 with a second washi tape color. You will have a large "+" sign across the table in two different colors.

5 Return to the first table top edge (Step 3) and the original washi tape roll, and press a strip of washi tape on either side of the first piece, connecting the corresponding pencil marks. Trim the tape at the edges.

6 Rotate the table one quarter turn and repeat Step 3 with a third washi tape color. Trim the tape at the edges.

7 Repeat Steps 5 and 6 two more times to create the woven effect on the finished table.

8 Coat the top of the table with the clear brush-on sealant for extra protection and durability. Let dry for 24 hours before using.

REMEMBER TO
BREATHE

Color
outside
the
lines

THE
FUTURE
IS
UNWRITTEN
— Joe Strummer

WASHI WALL FRAMES

Do you have a dull area of your wall with a little too much white space? This idea is going to thrill you, especially because you won't have to spend a lot of money. When you decide what you want to display, you won't have to shop for frames, because the washi tape *is* the frame! Simply hang your photos or art on the wall, then tape around them for an attractive solution to your white space woes.

SUPPLIES:

Printed photos or magazine clippings

Scissors or craft knife and self-healing cutting mat

Removable double-sided tape

Ruler or tape measure

Washi tape, in various colors and widths

Letter stickers (optional)

1 Trim your images as desired, and arrange them on the wall with double-sided tape.

2 Leaving a 1" margin, measure and stick a length of washi tape around all four sides to create a frame around each image. *Optional:* Use the scissors or the craft knife to miter the corners (page 13).

3 Create second frames around several of the first ones, for interest.

4 Create some empty frames on the wall and/or, in addition to the images, spell out a favorite saying or mantra in letter stickers.

SCRAPPY JAR STORAGE

Mason jars have incredible staying power in the craft and design world because of their appeal as a blank canvas for decorating *and* as a practical storage device—for all your pens, pencils, scissors, and binder clips—or razors, cotton balls, and toothbrushes! Good news: The surface responds well to washi tape, too. Cover your jars with a mishmash of tape scraps—this project is a perfect way to use up the end of a roll, or pick a theme and run with it.

SUPPLIES:

Glass jars

Washi tape, scrap pieces

Craft knife

1 Tear 1" strips of washi tape.

2 Press the tape pieces onto the sides of the glass jars, starting at the bottom and working up to the top.

3 Cover the jar completely. Cut through the washi tape around the neck of the jars with the craft knife to make a clean edge.

4 Trim the tape around the bottom of the jars to create clean edges there, too. Now fill them up!

TRY THIS NEXT:
Instead of using scraps, choose a few rolls in different shades of the same hue. Start at the bottom with the darkest shade and add lighter pieces as you move up the side of the jar for an ombré look.

COLORBLOCK WALL CLOCK

If you're busy like me, you might rely on a clock a lot—always keeping track of hours worked or deadlines or appointment times. Adding washi tape to a standard-issue clock instantly makes it a thousand times better looking, which makes the time pass all the more happily.

SUPPLIES:

Basic round wall clock

Screwdriver

Washi tape, in 2 coordinating colors

Craft knife

Foam brush

Decoupage medium, in matte or gloss finish

1 Use the screwdriver to open up the back of the clock and separate the frame, backing, and face.

2 Press a length of washi tape around the inside lip of the frame that sits behind the glass, overlapping the tape ends where they meet.

3 Reassemble the clock.

4 Using the same color washi tape from Step 2, and starting at the 12 o'clock position, press a piece of tape across the outer frame of the clock, from the glass to the edge of the frame.

5 Smooth down the tape, then trim it with the craft knife along the inner and outer edge of the frame.

6 Repeat Step 4 at 1 o'clock, 2 o'clock, and so on, until you reach 12 o'clock again.

7 Using the second washi tape color, cut three strips and press them onto the clock frame, in the spaces between each of the first tape strips. Start by filling in the space between 12 and 1 o'clock, pressing the washi tape from the front of the clock, over the top of the frame, to the back. Then move to the space between 1 and 2 o'clock.

8 Repeat with three more pieces of tape in each space, overlapping as necessary, until the last of the clock frame is covered.

9 Trim all of the excess washi tape around the clock frame edge (front and back) as necessary.

10 Paint decoupage medium over the taped portions of the clock to seal the tape in place.

11 Let dry, then hang the clock.

TRY THIS NEXT:
Punch individual dots of washi tape (see page 22) and press them onto the clock frame to make polka dots.

CHARMING CHORE CHART

When tasks like brushing teeth and doing homework and putting away toys need to be done on a massive scale, on a daily basis, how do you keep track? This handy chore chart will do—and the kids can help pick the washi colors and make it with you.

SUPPLIES:

Magnetic dry-erase board

Tape measure or ruler

Pencil

Washi tape, in at least 5 colors

Scissors

Large buttons or 1½" wooden discs

Magnets in the same diameter or smaller than buttons/discs

Hot glue gun

1 Determine how many chores to include on the chart, and add 1 to that number. (For example, if you would like five chores on your chart, six is your magic number.)

2 Use the tape measure to divide the board horizontally into your "magic number" (from Step 1) of evenly spaced rows. Mark each division with a pencil tick mark on each side.

3 Run strips of washi tape from left to right, connecting each pencil tick to its corresponding mark on the opposite edge.

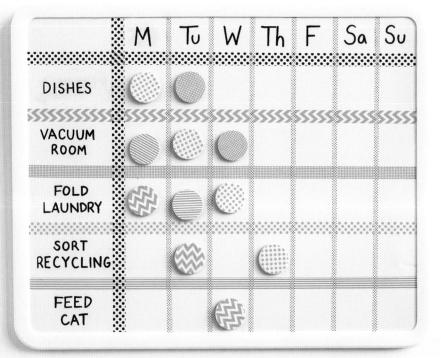

	M	Tu	W	Th	F	Sa	Su
DISHES	●	●					
VACUUM ROOM	●	●	●				
FOLD LAUNDRY	●	●	●				
SORT RECYCLING		●	●				
FEED CAT		●					

④ Measure and divide the board into nine evenly spaced vertical columns, making tick marks at the top and bottom edges.

⑤ Run strips of washi tape from top to bottom, connecting each pair of corresponding pencil ticks—except for the first pair, which you will ignore. The first section should be double the width of the other seven, since the first column will list the chore and the other seven will list the days of the week.

⑥ Select several large buttons or wooden discs that will be used to mark off chores, then hot-glue magnets to the back. Now, assign and conquer!

TRY THIS NEXT:
Make your own washi tape magnets using the technique on page 57.

WINNING WINDOW DECALS

Washi tape is a temporary solution on most surfaces, especially glass. This project takes that element of impermanence to a whole new level by turning washi into glass clings with the help of clear contact paper. We're basically talking about the mood ring of crafts: You can change the design on your window based on how you're feeling that day.

SUPPLIES:

Window

Clip art of silhouetted designs or shapes

Clear contact paper

Black marker

Washi tape

Scissors

1 Place the contact paper, backing side up, onto your work surface.

2 Place the selected clip art on top, and use the black marker to trace around it.

3 Turn the contact paper over and cover the shape using strips of washi tape, run vertically, horizontally, or diagonally.

4 Flip the contact paper back over and cut out the design.

5 Peel off the backing from the contact paper and stick to the window pane.

6 Repeat Steps 1 through 5 with your other designs and then organize them on glass as a mural!

DOLLAR STORE HOME DECOR VASES

Do you have a window ledge that needs a little something extra? There's no empty space that couldn't be improved with some fresh blooms. Here's the vessel to make that happen! Just grab some tired glassware (recycled works, too) and get washi taping. You're going to love the results.

SUPPLIES:

Glassware/jars (from a dollar store or dollar bins at your local craft store)

Enamel paint, in colors of your choice

Paintbrush

Washi tape, in 3 coordinating colors

Craft knife

1 Wash and dry the glassware.

2 Paint the insides of the jars using glass enamel paint if you intend to fill the vases with dry goods. Paint the outsides if you intend to fill the vases with water.

3 Center and press a strip of washi tape running vertically from the top to the bottom of a vase. Add a strip of coordinating tape parallel to and on either side of the strip.

Note: *On a smaller vase, three strips across may not fit. Locate the center, and place two strips vertically, about 1/8" from the vertical center line.*

4 Continue adding strips of tape until each vase has 2 to 3 parallel stripes down the front.

DOODLE DRY-ERASE BOARD

My boyfriend and I often leave romantic little notes for each other like "clean the bathroom" and "don't forget the dog food." Instead of digging around in drawers for scrap paper, here's a way to frame your next ask that's so sweet you might feel inspired to write an actual love note instead.

SUPPLIES:

Frame with a clear glass or plastic insert (from a dollar store)

White paper or cardstock (optional)

Washi tape, in a single color or monochromatic pattern

Scissors

Dry-erase marker

1 Remove the clear insert from the frame.

2 Cover the blank paper or cardboard insert with washi tape, running the tape vertically, horizontally, or diagonally. Line up the pattern of the washi tape as necessary to create a seamless pattern.

Note: *If the frame doesn't come with a paper insert, measure and cut one from white paper or cardstock.*

3 Use the scissors to trim the excess washi tape at the edges.

4 Put the clear insert in the frame, followed by the washi-taped insert.

5 Write your next love sonnet on the front with a dry-erase marker. When you need to erase it, use a dry paper towel or soft cloth.

BOHEMIAN BELT BUCKLE

Applying the washi tape and acrylic resin to a flat belt buckle is the easy part of this project. Perhaps the only hard part is the waiting: Although this project doesn't require a lot of time, it's spread out over three days to ensure proper drying. And it's worth it, because once your stylish new accessory *is* dry, it will be—and make you feel—positively invincible. Just make sure you plan ahead if you're making this for a special occasion! (Tip: Make them in bulk as personalized gifts for wedding attendants, book club friends, or sorority sisters.)

SUPPLIES:

Relatively flat belt buckle blank

Pencil

Vellum or scrap paper

Tape

White paper

Scissors

Washi tape

Paintbrushes

Decoupage medium, glossy finish

Acrylic resin

Embellishments: stickers, brads, rhinestones, glitter (optional)

Craft glue

1. Use a pencil and piece of vellum (or another scrap of paper) to trace or make a rubbing of the inside of the belt buckle.

2. Tape the tracing onto the white paper, and cut it out through both layers.

3. Press strips of washi tape onto the top of the white paper in a pattern of your choice. Use scissors to trim any excess tape along the edges.

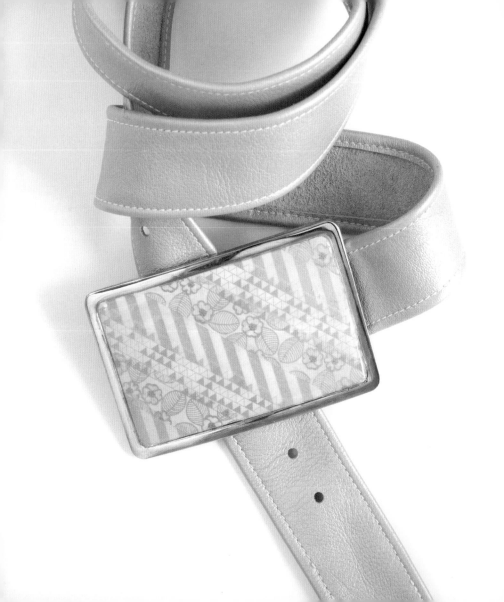

DECORATED DOOR

Doors are often ignored when it comes to home decor; they're typically expensive, and you wouldn't want to do something permanent that you may want to change later. Thanks to washi tape, you can finally give a door in your home some much-needed attention! This embellishment looks especially bright and cheery in a nursery or playroom.

SUPPLIES:

Door

Measuring tape

Pencil

Washi tape

Craft knife and self-healing cutting mat

1 Working from the top of the door down to the floor, measure and mark the vertical center of the door.

2 On each side of the center line, refer to the diagram (page 146) in order to mark symmetrical rectangles that mimic the panels of a wooden door.

Note: *If you are decorating a door that is already paneled, simply outline the panels with washi tape.*

3 Cut and place lengths of tape to cover the marked rectangles. Use the craft knife to miter the corners (see page 13).

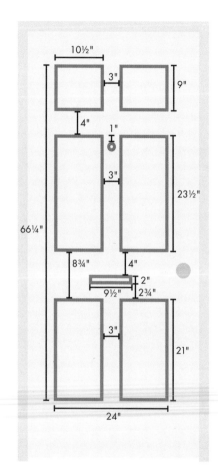

CHAPTER 4

JEWELRY AND FASHION

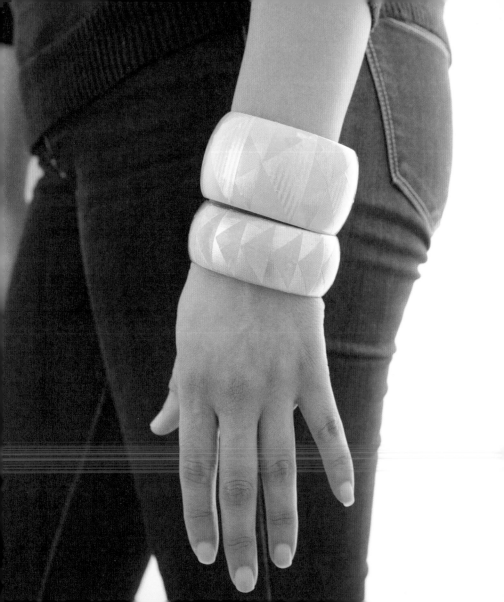

BOLD BANGLE BRACELETS

Do you ever start a project and then realize how much *fun* you're having doing it? Well, the fun meter is off the charts on this one. I warn you, though, I can't be responsible for time spent away from your children, significant other, or work duties to make these bracelets. But I promise you're going to have a blast.

SUPPLIES:

Wooden bangle bracelets

Paintbrushes

Acrylic paint, in color(s) of your choice

Washi tape, in 2 complementary colors or patterns

Wax paper

Pencil

Ruler

Craft knife and self-healing cutting mat

Decoupage medium

1 Paint the wooden bangles all one color, or paint the inside and/or the edges a different shade than the outside.

2 Tile together three strips of standard-width washi tape, overlapping them slightly, on a piece of wax paper. Measure and mark several isosceles triangles with a 1" base and several with a $\frac{1}{2}$" base.

3 Place the washi-taped wax paper on the cutting mat. Using the craft knife, cut out the triangles through both layers (wax paper and washi tape).

④ Peel the washi tape stickers from the wax paper and press them onto the bracelet, aligning the 1" triangles perpendicularly to the edge of the bracelet so that they look like arrows.

⑤ Paint on several coats of decoupage medium to seal the washi tape onto the bracelet and make it more durable. Let dry 24 hours before wearing.

TRY THIS NEXT:
For an alternative design, alternate 1" triangles with a pair of ½" triangles side by side—as shown in the top bracelet in the photo on page 148.

4 Paint decoupage medium onto the back of the paper and press it into the belt buckle blank. Let it dry for 15 to 20 minutes.

5 One layer at a time, and letting each dry overnight, add three layers of acrylic resin. After each layer has been applied, let the resin dry completely in a warm place (to prevent cracking). *Optional:* Embed any desired embellishments in the third layer, so they can add dimension and texture to the buckle.

6 Once the third layer of resin on the buckle is completely dry, attach it to a belt.

DESIGNER SHADES

It's nice to have choices when it comes to sunglasses, especially when coordinating your entire look. Browse your local dollar store to get some basic frames, then simply add washi tape! If you happen to lose or break the frames, you can easily replace them and repeat the process.

SUPPLIES:

Sunglasses

Washi tape

Craft knife and self-healing cutting mat

Paintbrush

Decoupage medium

1 Press a strip of washi tape along one of the stems of the sunglasses.

Note: *You may need more than one strip depending on the thickness of the stems and the width of the washi tape.*

2 Smooth the washi tape, then place the stem of your sunglasses tape side down onto the cutting mat. Carefully trim the excess washi tape around the edges with a craft knife.

3 Repeat Steps 1 and 2 on the other stem of the sunglasses.

4 Smooth any loose edges with your fingers, making sure the washi tape is secure.

5 For a more permanent seal, paint decoupage medium over each stem, and let it dry.

DIY ENVELOPE CLUTCH

Find a plastic envelope at the office superstore, add washi tape, and you'll have a stylish new clutch fit for a Saturday night out on the town. Done!

SUPPLIES:

Clear poly envelope (found online or at office supply stores)

Washi tape, in 2 complementary colors

Scissors

Craft knife

Paintbrush

Decoupage medium

Button

Needle and thread

1 Press a length of washi tape horizontally around the base of the envelope at the bottom.

2 Align a second piece of the same tape directly above the first and wrap it around. Continue to press strips of tape horizontally along the envelope until you reach the opening. Tape over any Velcro or snap closures.

3 Trim the excess tape along the edge, and use the craft knife to cut around any closures you taped over in Step 2.

4 Use the second color of washi tape to accent each edge and cover the envelope flap, as shown.

5 Paint decoupage medium over the washi tape to prevent it from peeling up. Let it dry.

6 Sew a button onto the envelope flap as a faux closure. (You may need to pierce through the Velcro with the tip of the craft knife to do this.)

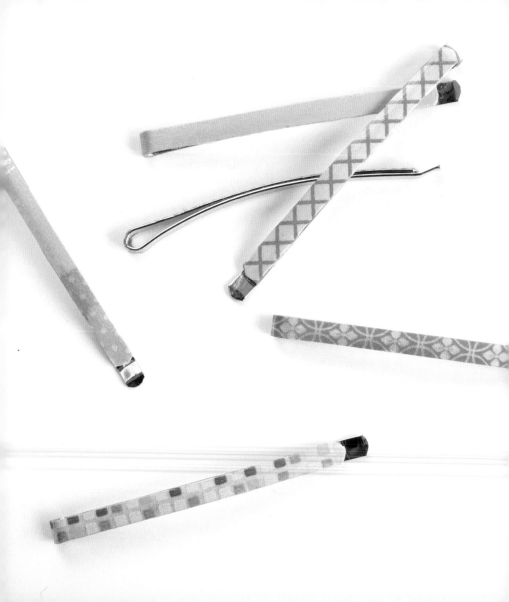

HANDSOME HAIR CLIPS

If you have hair that is as independent as you are, sometimes the only way to keep it in line is with clips. These basic ones are all dressed up with washi tape. They're perfect for children, too—surprise them with a pattern you pick, or let them choose their own!

SUPPLIES:

Silver hairpins

Washi tape, in a variety of patterns

Scissors

Paintbrush

Decoupage medium, sparkle or regular finish

1 Select several washi tape patterns, and press a strip of tape along the top of each hairpin.

2 Trim the excess tape around the edges with scissors, and smooth down the edges of the tape on all sides.

3 Coat the tape with several layers of decoupage medium to seal it, then let dry thoroughly before wearing the clips.

PLAYFUL PINWHEEL EARRINGS

I came up with the idea for these playful earrings in the wood section of the craft store one day, feeling inspired by all the mini wood shapes. The funnest part is the itty-bitty pinwheel on front of the discs. I can't think of a more brilliant gift idea—and you can knock out several pairs in one sitting.

SUPPLIES:

Two ½" wooden circles, preferably with holes drilled through

Drill with ³⁄₃₂" mini drill bit (if the wooden circles do not have holes already)

Ruler

Pencil

White piece of paper

Scissors

Washi tape

Craft glue

Mini rhinestone or other small embellishment (optional)

2 jump rings

Round-nose pliers

2 French hook ear wires

1 If there isn't a hole in the wooden discs already, use the drill to make a hole about ⅛" from the edge of each of the wooden circles.

2 Measure and mark two 1" squares onto white paper, then cut them out. Edge the squares with washi tape cut about ¹⁄₁₆" to ⅛" wide. Trim the edges.

3 Fold and crease the paper in half diagonally in two directions so that the paper is divided into four triangles.

4 Using the fold lines as a guide, measure and mark ¼" from the center along each crease.

5 Using the fold lines again as a guide, cut from each corner toward the center of the square, stopping at the marks made in Step 4.

6 Squeeze a small dot of glue in the center of the square, and gently roll each of the four corners into the center of the pinwheel without creasing them.

7 Repeat with the second paper square to make a second pinwheel. Let dry. *Optional:* Add a small rhinestone or other embellishment at the center of each pinwheel.

8 Assemble the earrings by passing a jump ring through each hole, then using the round-nose pliers to pry open, attach, and close a French hook ear wire.

9 Glue a pinwheel to the front of each wooden circle. Let dry.

CHARMED BRACELET

My mother and I have charm bracelet collections and love finding—or making!—each other new charms. The talented and adventurous designer was sweet enough to share her tutorial here. The result is something unexpected and surprisingly durable.

SUPPLIES:

Charm bracelet blank with clasp

Washi tape, in bright colors

Foil sheets

Sizzix Big Shot machine and
  Sizzix BIGZ die 3-D flowers*

Bamboo skewer

Jewelry glue

Decoupage medium

20-gauge wire

Ruler

Wire cutters

Round-nose pliers

Flush cutters

Coordinating beads and charms

*Note: *If you don't have a die-cut machine, use the Wrapped Flower tutorial on page 24 to build your base flowers.*

1 Apply washi tape in slightly overlapping strips onto both sides of a foil sheet.

2 Use the Sizzix Big Shot machine to die-cut a small rose shape using Sizzix BIGZ die 3-D flowers from the tape-covered foil.

3 Roll the diecut around a bamboo skewer to create a rose shape. Place a dab of glue on the inner center of the flower, holding the coiled shape in place until it grabs.

4 Repeat Steps 2 and 3 until you have created 5 or 6 flowers.

5 Dip the flowers into decoupage medium to seal them. Let them dry.

6 To connect the flowers to the bracelet, cut 4" to 5" lengths of 20-gauge wire. Then coil one end to create a 3/8" diameter surface for gluing to the back of the rose.

Note: *Begin the coil with round-nose pliers and finish with your fingers.*

7 Once the coil is about 3/8" in diameter, bend the wire 90 degrees just a couple of millimeters above the edge of the rose.

8 Form the 90-degree bend into a 1/8" wire loop using the round-nose pliers. Slide the open loop onto a link on a bracelet-length chain with clasps, then wrap the end of the wire around the stem between the loop and the coil on the back of the rose to secure it. Use the flush cutters to trim off any excess wire.

9 Add coordinating beads and charms as desired.

MAKE IT MODERN PENDANT

What does a crafty lady do when she can't find the perfect piece of jewelry to pair with a new dress? She makes one! The variety in washi tape—muted or bold colors, quiet or playful patterns—makes it impossible not to be able to strike the right tone. To the washi tape stash!

SUPPLIES:

1" pendant base with acrylic dome

Washi tape, in at least 2 complementary colors or patterns

White cardstock

1" circle punch

Paintbrush

Decoupage medium

Jewelry glue

Necklace chain

1 Press two complementary washi tape strips side by side onto the cardstock.

2 Use the 1" punch to cut a few circles from the taped cardstock.

3 Paint the top of the taped circles with decoupage medium, then press the acrylic dome over it. Let it dry.

4 Adhere the back of the circle into the pendant base using jewelry glue. Let it dry.

5 Once the pendant is completely dry, string it onto the chain. It's ready to wear!

TROMP L'OEIL FAUX-POCKET TEE

Revamp a plain, old T-shirt with a cool washi tape design! Why not? Fashion doesn't always have to be serious. Go for a simple pocket outline and choose the washi tape for its pattern. Now think: What else can you put a faux pocket on?

SUPPLIES:

White or light-colored V-neck T-shirt (with no pocket), in cotton or cotton blend

Washi tape, in narrow width

White paper

Scissors

Computer with scanner and printer

Iron-on sheet

Iron

1 Use the washi tape to "draw" a pocket shape onto the white paper that is proportionate to the T-shirt.

2 Trim the ends with scissors so that the corners of the pocket are clean and sharp.

3 Scan the design and print it onto an iron-on sheet.

4 Cut out the pocket shape from the iron-on sheet, leaving no margin around the edge of the tape.

5 Try on the T-shirt to determine the correct placement for the pocket. Remove the shirt and arrange the pocket on the front of the shirt.

6 Following the instructions on the packaging, iron the pocket onto the T-shirt.

GLAMOUR RINGS

For those days when you're craving a little fancy in your life, rings are one of the quickest answers. Ring blanks are available in mass quantities at the craft store, and they're incredibly easy to doll up—in just a few hours you can have a collection of new jewelry for yourself or to give as gifts.

SUPPLIES:

Ring blanks with dimensional acrylic shapes

Washi tape

White cardstock

Paintbrush

Decoupage medium, in glossy finish

Craft knife and self-healing cutting mat

Jewelry glue

1 Press strips of washi tape next to each other onto the cardstock, lining up elements of the tape's design to create a continuous pattern.

2 Paint the top of the tape with decoupage medium, then press the desired acrylic shape over the top. Let it dry.

3 Trace around the acrylic shape with the craft knife to trim the excess cardstock and tape.

4 Paint the back of the piece with decoupage medium, then let it dry.

5 Use jewelry glue to attach the back of the shapes to the ring blanks. Let dry for 24 hours before wearing.

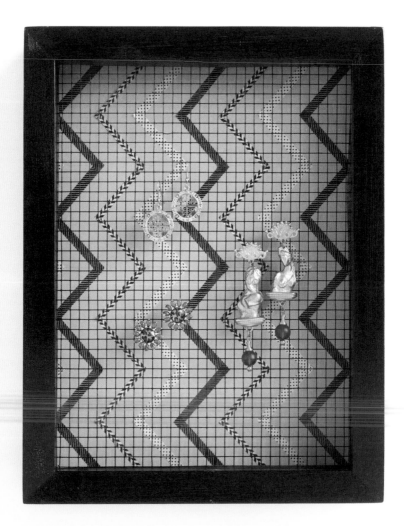

JEWELRY HANGER

If a jewelry box isn't your style, try a storage method that's all about showing off your collection. You can size it to fit your needs based on the number of pieces you'd like to display; simply adjust the dimensions of the frame.

SUPPLIES:

Washi tape, in 3 patterns

Wooden shadow box

Ruler

Pencil

Roll of fine mesh (like a screen) or burlap ("hardware cloth")

Wire cutters

Staple gun

Cardstock

Scissors

1 Remove the back of the shadow box, then the frame layers and glass at the front.

2 Mark the dimensions of the frame onto the wire mesh. Use the wire cutters to cut out the rectangle.

3 Insert the mesh rectangle and staple it to the inside of the frame.

4 Measure the back of the shadow box, then mark the dimensions onto the cardstock and cut it out.

5 Measure and mark a geometric design onto the cardstock, then "trace" over the design with strips of washi tape. Trim any excess tape.

6 Place the cardstock into the shadow box frame and replace the back. (You won't need the glass.)

7 Hang the frame on the wall, and insert earring hooks into the mesh.

HEADBAND DU JOUR

The headband is a classic hair accessory that's both practical and stylish—and when you DIY it with the help of a nearly limitless supply of washi tape patterns, you can cater the design to any style you want to rock, be it preppy, punk, mod, vintage, sporty, nerdy . . . you get the idea!

SUPPLIES:

Headband (flat ones work best)

Washi tape, in at least 2 complementary patterns or colors

Scissors

Paintbrush

Decoupage medium

1 Start at one end of the headband and wrap a strip of tape diagonally across the top of it.

2 Trim the tape with scissors, then fold the ends of the strip of tape to the back of the band.

3 Repeat Steps 1 and 2 with another strip of tape. Continue alternating the colored strips until the entire headband is covered.

4 Paint a coat of decoupage medium over the entire band to seal the tape. Allow it to dry completely before wearing!

WOODEN WONDER BEAD NECKLACE

Wooden beads are materials that harken back to childhood craft projects. But when washi tape enters the mix, a necklace of simple wooden shapes is elevated to a more sophisticated plane. Customize the beads to match a particular outfit, or pair them with an all-black ensemble for a colorful statement piece.

SUPPLIES:

Wooden beads

Paintbrushes

Acrylic paint, in colors of your choice

Washi tape

Craft knife

Decoupage medium

Necklace chain or silk cord thin enough to string through the beads

1 Paint the wooden beads and let them dry.

2 Tear off several small pieces of washi tape and press them, one at a time, lengthwise along the side of the bead, layering colors as desired. Smooth the tape, cajoling it around any rounded or faceted surfaces.

3 Carefully trim the tape around the bead holes with the craft knife.

4 Repeat Steps 2 and 3 on each wooden bead.

5 Paint a layer of decoupage medium over the beads to seal the tape, then let them dry.

6 String the beads onto the necklace chain or silk cord to wear.

POPSICLE STICK BRACELETS

This is a fun craft that uses basic supplies but will keep children busy during summer or winter break dry spells. Yep, you can turn a flat wooden stick into a bracelet with water—amazing, right? But you have to prep a few days ahead. Once you make the bracelet, the children can decorate the band any way they like.

SUPPLIES:

Large wooden craft sticks (tongue depressors)

Tall glass of water (for soaking)

Mug (for molding)

Washi tape

Decoupage medium

Paintbrush

Awl or piercing tool and self-healing cutting mat

Hemp beading cord, #20 gauge

Scissors

1 Fully immerse the sticks in water, and let soak for at least two days, until they are pliable enough to mold. *Tip:* Cover them with a plate to keep them submerged, otherwise they will float to the top.

2 Once they are pliable, pull the sticks out of the water and begin carefully molding them into a bracelet shape. Bend them very slowly—any fast moves, and they will break.

3 Place the molded sticks in the mug, and allow them to dry in the sun for 1 day. *Note:* If there's no access to sunlight, leave the sticks to dry for 2 days in order to set fully.

4 Wrap strips of washi tape along the length of one of the bracelets,

wrapping the tape around the ends of the bracelet to the inside.

⑤ Fold the sides of the washi tape around the sides of the bracelet to the inside.

⑥ Press a strip of tape to line the inside of the bracelet, catching the edges of the folded-over washi tape underneath to make a seamless inside surface.

⑦ Paint a layer of decoupage medium over the tape to prevent it from peeling. Let it dry.

⑧ Using the awl, pierce holes through both ends of the bracelet, about $\frac{1}{4}$" to $\frac{3}{8}$" in from the end.

Note: It's okay if the wood cracks a bit—it will make it easier to pull the cord through.

⑨ Thread a length of cord through each hole, securing it with a knot.

⑩ Slip the bracelet around the wrist, and tie the cords to secure.

TRY THIS NEXT:
Make a matching pair of bracelets so you can keep one and give one—a fresh take on the classic friendship bracelet.

CUSTOM NAIL ART

When I learned that you could customize your nails with washi tape, it opened up a whole new world for me! It's easy to mix and match colors, the drying time is shorter than a traditional manicure, it'll never chip, and with my large collection of washi rolls, I could have a different manicure and pedicure every day for the next 10 years. Okay, maybe not that long, but I can definitely match my nails to my outfits with fun patterns. And even better, when you want to change up your look, you can just peel the washi tape off in one piece!

SUPPLIES:

Clear nail polish base coat

Washi tape

Pencil

Mini scissors or craft knife and self-healing cutting mat

Wax paper

Clear nail polish top coat

Mini punch, for making ¼" dots or other shapes (optional)

1 Make sure your nails are clean and dry, then paint them with a base coat and let them dry completely.

2 Tear off a piece of washi tape and press it over your nail. With a pencil, trace along the edge of your nail to make an impression on the tape.

3 Peel the washi tape piece off your nail and carefully cut out the traced shape using scissors or the craft knife.

181

④ Press the tape back onto your fingernail, smooth it down, and add a top coat over the tape. Let it dry. *Optional:* Press a length of washi tape in a complementary color or pattern onto wax paper and punch out shapes. Then peel the washi-taped shape off the wax paper and press it onto the nail design before adding a top coat.

⑤ Repeat Steps 2 through 4 on each of your fingernails.

⑥ Add a second top coat over each fingernail design and let it dry completely.

TRY THIS NEXT:
Use washi tape as a stencil! Either use a punch to create cutouts or fold the tape in half, snip a shape on the fold (such as half of a heart), and unfold the tape to reveal the shape. Then smooth the cutout or shape onto the nail design. Paint over the stencil with colored nail polish. Just before the polish dries, pull up and remove the washi tape stencil to reveal the design underneath. Add a top coat to seal it.

WASHI BROOCH BOUQUET

Here's a project to turn those two-dimensional strips of washi tape loveliness into three-dimensional, bendable blooms. To finish, put a cluster of the buds together with a pin to make a pretty brooch.

SUPPLIES:

26-gauge floral wire

Wire cutters/pliers

Ruler

Pencil or marker

Washi tape

Scissors

Wire flower stamens

Floral tape

Jewelry glue

Metal pin back

1 To make the flowers, cut five 6" lengths of wire, one length per flower petal.

2 Find the center of each piece of wire and wrap it around a pencil or marker (or other rounded object less than the diameter of the width of your washi tape) to create petal loops. Adjust each wire loop to the preferred petal shape.

3 Cut a piece of washi tape a little more than twice the length of the petal loop. Place the loop onto the lower half of tape and fold the remaining tape over. Press the layers together firmly. Trim off the excess washi tape corners to create petal shapes.

4 To make a leaf, repeat Steps 1 through 3, but use only a 3" section of wire without a loop, and trim the excess tape into a leaf shape.

5 Turn the leaf wire and repeat Step 4, making a leaf at the opposite end of the wire. Fold the double-leaf wire in half.

6 Repeat Steps 1 through 3 and Steps 4 through 5 as desired to create various sizes and shapes for different color and patterned flowers.

7 Fold two stamens in half and place 5 flower petals around them.

8 Wrap the petals and stamens tightly together with floral tape, beginning at the base of the petals. Wrap the tape around the wires several times before adding leaves.

9 Place the folded portion of the wire leaves against the flower stem and continue tightly wrapping with floral tape. Wrap to the end of the wires and just slightly beyond before tearing off the end of the tape to finish.

10 Separate and bend the flower petals and leaves to desired shapes.

11 Repeat to create as many flowers as desired. Cluster them together using the floral tape.

12 Glue the flower bundle to a pin back. Let dry completely before wearing.

CHAPTER 5

HOLIDAYS AND CELEBRATIONS

PRETTY PARTY CUPS AND SPOONS

Some parties (or all, if you're so inclined) call for a thought-out theme and color story. If you want to have everything match—down to the dessert cups and spoons—add washi tape! Your guests will squeal and tell you how much they love the color coordination—plus it's just plain fun!

SUPPLIES:

Wooden spoons

Paper frozen dessert cups

Washi tape, in various complementary colors

Scissors

1 Start at the base of the handle on one of the spoons and press a piece of washi along the handle, trimming the end of the tape at the end of the handle. *Optional:* Press another piece of washi tape onto the back of the handle.

2 Repeat Step 1 on the remaining spoons.

3 For the cups, cut a clean edge on a washi tape roll and, starting at the top of the cup (under the lip), roll a length of tape vertically down the side. Trim the tape when you reach the bottom.

4 Repeat Step 3 using additional washi tapes, until the cup is covered.

5 Repeat Steps 3 and 4 as desired to cover additional cups.

NO-SEW, NO-GLUE PARTY BUNTING

This bunting banner makes a lovely decoration for any special occasion, such as weddings or garden parties. But why not hang it as any everyday room trimming? A lot of banners you see out there require sewing and gluing, but not this one. Just grab your scissors and washi tape, and you'll be party ready in no time.

SUPPLIES:

Washi tape, several rolls in the colors of your choice

Ruler

Scissors

Clear tape (optional)

Baker's twine

1 Cut four washi tape strips each about 8" long. Lay them down, slightly overlapping, onto your work surface, sticky side up. *Optional:* Use clear tape to temporarily tack down the ends of the strips.

2 Place a piece of baker's twine down the center (perpendicular to the tape pieces, and leaving a trail of twine at least 12" long to one side). Gently release the washi tape from the mat, and fold it over the twine and onto itself.

3 Repeat Steps 1 and 2 about every 4" along the twine. Continue until the banner is the desired length.

4 On each pennant, use the scissors to cut a triangle shape from the end of the washi tape to create a dovetail detail.

5 Make a knot at each end of the bunting, and hang it.

PUNCHED-UP PARTY HATS

A lot of the party hats available these days are either a solid color, which is kind of boring, or come preprinted with commercial characters. If you aren't having a character-themed party, there aren't a lot of good options! But if you buy hats in solid colors and then customize them with washi tape, you'll have the best party hats ever—and all your friends will be asking where you got them.

SUPPLIES:

Plain paper party hats

Washi tape

Tape measure or ruler

Scissors

3" square of cardboard

Thin twine (like embroidery floss)

Hot glue gun

1 Press a strip of washi tape that extends diagonally from the base of the hat. Let it follow the natural curve of the hat until it meets itself (trim it) or the edge of the hat (fold the end inside the hat, or trim it at the bottom).

2 Repeat Step 1 on the same hat, starting each strip parallel to the first and wrapping until there are about 3-5 strips of tape wrapped around the cone.

3 Repeat Steps 1 and 2 as many times as there are hats to decorate.

4 To make the sprays for the top of each hat, fold a 3' strip of washi tape in half lengthwise, adhesive side in. Cut it lengthwise, to make 2 thin strips.

5 Hold the ends of the strips together and wrap them around the 3" piece of cardboard. Use a piece of tape to hold them in place temporarily.

6 Thread a piece of twine through the loops of washi tape at one end of the card and tie a knot around the strands. Cut through the strands at the opposite end.

7 Wrap a strip of washi tape around the doubled-over, knotted end. Then trim the "fringe" to a uniform length.

8 Hot-glue a washi spray to the top of each hat, and let dry before wearing.

TRY THIS NEXT:
Go vertical! Press 5 or 6 evenly spaced strips of tape from the top of the cone to the bottom.

PERFECT PACKAGE GIFT BOW

When it comes to gift wrapping, kraft paper turns out to be the perfect blank slate for embellishing—with stickers, markers, paint, ribbons, or . . . washi tape! These bows are a delightful combination of two qualities that make a standout washi tape project: They are simple to make, and they make a big impact. And as an added bonus, these gift bows are durable enough that they can be reused!

SUPPLIES:

Washi tape

Ruler

Hot glue gun or double-sided tape

Brad (with extra-long prongs—the office supply variety)

Wrapped present

1 Press two strips of washi tape together, sticky sides in, to create one ribbon strip. For one gift bow, make:

a. 3 ribbon strips, each $8^{1}/_{2}$" long

b. 3 ribbon strips, each $7^{1}/_{2}$" long

c. 2 ribbon strips, each $6^{1}/_{2}$" long

d. 1 ribbon strip that is $3^{1}/_{2}$" long

2 Twist ribbon strips **a** through **c** into the shape of an infinity symbol (or figure eight), and secure the ends with hot glue or double-sided tape.

3 Form a circle with the smallest ribbon strip (d) and secure it to itself.

4 Beginning with the smallest figure-eight shape (*not* the circle from Step 3), punch the brad through both layers at its center, where the washi tape makes an X. Then punch through the remaining figure-eight shapes, layering as you go.

5 When you're done, fold back the ends of the brad to secure the layers.

6 Attach the small circle to the center of each bow with hot glue or double-sided tape.

7 Secure the bow to the wrapped package with hot glue or double-sided tape.

FAUX FLORAL BOUQUET

Add a whimsical touch to a wedding or other event by creating a washi tape bouquet that is memorable and lasting. Choose the number and size of blooms depending on the event: For wedding centerpieces, go with more and larger blooms; for a smaller party, make mini bouquets to display in small glass vases.

SUPPLIES:

Washi tape, in various widths and in 8 or 9 colors (1 for each flower)

Ruler

Pencil

Decorative scissors

Floral wire

Hot glue gun

Floral tape

Scissors

1 Cut two 12"-long strips of washi tape in the same color, then sandwich them together, sticky side in.

2 Use the decorative scissors to cut along the edge of one of the long sides.

3 Roll the tape strip around one end of a piece of floral wire (the stem) to form a bloom. Use hot glue to secure the "petals" as needed.

4 Wrap the floral tape down the length of the floral wire, stretching as you go to activate the tape.

5 Repeat Steps 1 through 4 for the desired number of flowers.

6 Arrange the flowers into a bouquet, and secure it with the floral tape.

7 Trim the stems as desired.

VALENTINE GIFT BOXES

I save cardboard rolls for all kinds of craft projects—and pillow boxes are high on the list. Candy is one of those tried-and-true Valentine gifts, and these are *the* way to present the sweets.

SUPPLIES:

Toilet paper tubes

Decorative paper

Double-sided adhesive

Scissors

Washi tape

Pencil

White cardstock

Small hole punch

Baker's twine

1 Wrap the toilet paper tubes with decorative paper, using the double-sided adhesive to secure it. Trim the excess at each end of the tubes.

2 Fold washi tape around the raw edges of each tube to cover them.

3 Use a pencil to draw some valentine-themed shapes onto the cardstock.

4 Flip it over so the pencil markings aren't visible, and cover the back with strips of washi tape.

5 Cut out the shapes, then punch a hole at the top of each.

6 Press gently on each tube to flatten it slightly. Insert treats into the center of the tubes, and fold the edges of the tube in on both ends.

7 Wrap baker's twine around the length of the tube and string a few shapes onto it before knotting, and trimming the ends.

EASTER EGG WREATH

This sweet wreath is more modern than your standard fare, and endlessly customizable. Hang it on your door or over the mantel to usher in spring!

SUPPLIES:

25 unfinished oval wooden pieces (about 1½" × 3")

Paintbrushes

Acrylic paint, in white

MDF flat wreath form

Scissors

Washi tape

Craft knife and self-healing cutting mat

Decoupage medium

Hot glue gun

Ribbon

1 Paint all the wooden pieces and the wreath form white.

2 Cut the washi tape into various patterns and press them onto the fronts of the wooden pieces in a design similar to one you'd use to decorate real Easter eggs.

3 Paint decoupage medium over the front of the wooden pieces. Let dry.

4 Hot-glue the wooden pieces to the wreath form.

5 Cut an 18"–24" piece of ribbon. Loop it, and attach it to the back of the form using hot glue. Let it cool for several hours before hanging.

TRY THIS NEXT:
Forget messy dyes—decorate all your Easter eggs with washi tape!

PAPER PARTY LANTERNS

Party decor isn't always the easiest or cheapest thing to come up with. You can end up spending hundreds of dollars on ambience alone, and that's before any of the food or favors! Paper lanterns are only a few dollars, so you can customize to your heart's desire.

SUPPLIES:

Paper lantern(s)

Washi tape, in at least 2 coordinating patterns

Tape measure or ruler

8" piece of cardboard

Embroidery floss

Scissors

Tapestry needle

1 First, create the tassels (one for each lantern). Fold a 3' strip of washi tape in half lengthwise, adhesive side in. Cut it lengthwise, to make 2 thin strips.

2 Hold the ends of the strips together and wrap them 20 times around the 8" piece of cardboard, temporarily holding them in place with a piece of tape.

3 Thread a tapestry needle with 12" of embroidery floss. Thread the needle through the loops of washi tape at one end of the card and tightly tie a knot around the strands. Cut through the strands at the opposite end and remove the bundle from the cardboard.

4 Wrap a piece of washi tape around the tassel about 1" to 1¼" from the knotted end (the top). Trim the tassel fringe so the strands are even. Set it aside.

⑤ Unfold the paper lantern and press a length of washi tape vertically from the opening at the top (wrap the end of the tape around the edge to the inside to anchor it) to the opening at the bottom.

⑥ Repeat Step 5 on the opposite side of the lantern with the same tape (this should visually split the lantern in half along the vertical axis).

⑦ Press two more lengths of tape halfway between the first two pieces so the four pieces of tape visually split the lantern into quarters.

⑧ Select a second washi tape pattern and place evenly spaced strips between the four original strips. (Depending on the size of the lantern and the width of the tape, you may add or subtract strips of tape as desired.)

⑨ Tie the thread attached to the tassel to the wire at the base of the lantern.

⑩ Repeat to create multiple lanterns.

TRY THIS NEXT:
Instead of stripes, snip small squares of washi and place them around the outside of the lantern to look like confetti.

AWARD-WINNING RIBBON

It's important to give ourselves a little pat on the back for a job well done from time to time. You really don't need a particular occasion to make these ribbons, but they make the recipient feel like she did on field day in the first grade. (Ahem! Long jump winner right here!) These washi award ribbons make perfect party favors—and you can personalize them for each guest!

SUPPLIES:

2½" wooden circle, 1 per ribbon

Acrylic paint, in various colors to coordinate with the washi tape

Paintbrush

Washi tape, in various colors

Scissors

Computer with a word-processing program and a printer

Printer paper

Clear acrylic spray, in matte finish (optional)

2" hole punch

Hot glue gun

Metal pin backs

1 Paint the wooden circle(s), then let it (them) dry.

2 Unroll three 5" strips of washi tape onto your work surface, sticky side up.

3 Align and press a 5" strip on top of each (sticky sides in).

4 Cut a small triangle or V shape from one end of each strip so that each ribbon piece ends in a dovetail shape.

5 Repeat Steps 1 through 4 to create as many ribbons as desired.

GRAND PRIZE

WINNER

1st

6 Open a word-processing program and type the name of the award. Size it as necessary to fit into a 2" circle, and leave a healthy margin so you'll have room to trim and punch.

7 Print the text onto printer paper.

8 Press strips of washi tape over the text on the paper. Smooth it thoroughly, then feed the same sheet of paper with washi tape on it back through the printer.

9 Give the ink a few minutes to set. *Optional:* Spray with a clear matte acrylic spray to help it set.

10 Trim roughly around the text so there's room to fit the hole punch. Then insert each piece of paper into the circle punch with the words oriented so the text is visible. Center the text in the window, then press down.

11 Hot-glue the punched circle onto the front of a painted circle.

12 Hot-glue a pin back to the center back of the circle. Then glue the uncut ends of the three ribbons of washi tape, arranging them at different angles, below the pin back. Let them cool.

FAVOR TAKE-OUT BOXES

Chinese food take-out containers might quickly turn into one of your most prized projects, once you try making a few of these. It's easy to personalize these boxes with your (or your guest's) favorite letter, shape, or symbol—and anyone will love taking a favor home in one of these cute boxes.

SUPPLIES:

Cardboard take-out containers in the color of your choice

Washi tape, in 2 solid colors and 1 coordinating pattern

Scissors (optional)

Candy or other treats

1 Select the solid washi tape colors and press strips of it onto one side of the box as the base to your design. Tear or trim the ends with scissors.

2 Press the second (patterned) tape over the first, adding stripes or hand-torn dots as desired in the shape of your design.

3 Continue placing tape until the entire letter, shape, or symbol is complete.

4 Fill the container with treats, candy, or whatever else you like.

FESTIVE VOTIVE HOLDERS

Small tea lights are a must for any party or gathering. They are very inexpensive, and you can place them down the center of a table to complete your look. Decorating one with washi tape takes just a few seconds, so you can have fun experimenting with different colors and patterns until you find exactly what suits your atmosphere.

SUPPLIES:

Tea light candles

Washi tape, in a variety of colors, in standard widths

Craft knife and self-healing cutting mat

Ruler

Pencil

Note: *Be sure that no washi tape extends above the edge of the votive. And, for safety, never leave an open flame unattended.*

1 Cut 5" long strips of washi tape, one for each votive.

2 Wrap a strip of washi tape around the outside of each votive, covering the metal base completely and overlapping the ends at the back.

TRY THIS NEXT:
Cut small triangles from a complementary color washi tape and apply them to the votive sideways as arrows, or extending down from the top edge as bunting.

PARTY MASK

Washi tape is typically used in two-dimensional ways, and that's what I love about this fun, feathery project: It's 3-D! Use a store-bought mask as the base—or fashion your own! You'll be the hit of your next masquerade party.

SUPPLIES:

Washi tape

Scissors

Ruler

Pencil

Floral wire

Hot glue gun

Mask blank

Sequins

Dowel rod

1 Cut a 4" strip of washi tape. Press a length of floral wire about halfway onto the strip of tape and fold the tape in half, over the wire.

2 Use scissors to trim the washi tape into a feather shape around the edges, with the wire acting as the shaft of the feather.

3 Cut diagonal lines into the washi tape to mimic the "vane" of a feather. Ruffle some of the pieces.

4 Repeat Steps 3 through 5 to create more feathers.

5 Hot-glue the feathers to the front of the mask, working around the perimeter in toward the eyes.

6 Glue sequins around the eyes and at random places on the mask.

7 Wrap the dowel rod in washi tape. Then glue the top of the rod to the back of the mask, $\frac{1}{2}$" from one side.

MOONLIT MUMMY LANTERNS

Add an eerie but playful effect to your holiday decor with these easy mummy lanterns. If you dig the jars out of your recycling bin, you'll spend next to nothing on this project. Drop an LED tea light inside for a haunted effect!

SUPPLIES:

Glass jars

Spray paint, in silver or mirror finish

Spray bottle with a solution of 1 part vinegar, 1 part water

Paper towels

Washi tape, in white

Hot glue gun

Googly eyes, in various sizes

LED tea lights

1 Apply a light coat of silver spray paint to the outside of the glass jars. Immediately spray with the vinegar solution. Let dry for one minute.

2 Apply spray paint again, then let dry for 3 to 5 minutes. Dab the wet areas gently with dry paper towels to create a mercury glass effect.

3 Repeat Steps 1 and 2 until the jars are covered. Multiple coats may be added until the desired finish is achieved. Let dry completely.

4 Wrap the white washi tape randomly around the jar, leaving silver paint exposed, to resemble mummy wrapping.

5 Hot-glue two googly eyes next to each other, about 1½"–2" from the top of the jar, and drop in an LED tea light.

SPOOKY TREAT BAGS

We all know what's going inside those treat bags—candy!—so we'll concentrate our fun on the outside. Don't be limited by any preconceived notions of "Halloween colors"—beyond the traditional black and orange, purple or green can make a pretty spooky showing, too! And don't forget: Day of the Dead is traditionally celebrated with all sorts of bright hues, including pink and yellow.

SUPPLIES:

Small black treat bags

Washi tape, in at least 3 Halloween colors and patterns

Scissors

1 Open a bag and wrap the washi tape horizontally around all four sides.

2 Repeat with the two additional patterns of washi tape.

3 Use the scissors to cut small jagged triangles in the top edge of the bag, all the way across.

4 Repeat Steps 1 through 3 for all bags. Fill with tissue paper and candy, and keep an ear out for trick-or-treaters!

JACK-O'-LAMP

The best holiday decorations are ones that can be used year after year and you can file this project into the forever category. Pumpkins obviously don't last, but this jack-o'-lantern lamp will.

SUPPLIES:

Glass table lamp, such as the Lykta from Ikea

Clip art of silhouetted jack-o'-lantern face

Craft knife and self-healing cutting mat

Wax paper

Stencil tape

Washi tape, in orange

Tweezers

1 Place the selected clip art on the cutting mat. Lay a piece of wax paper over it, securing the corners with stencil tape.

2 Press strips of washi tape horizontally onto the wax paper, over the clip art. Overlap each preceding strip at least ⅛". Repeat until the jack-o'-lantern face is covered.

3 Use the clip art as a guide to cut out the jack-o'-lantern eyes, nose, and mouth. You should have four separate washi tape stickers: two eyes, one nose, and a mouth.

4 Peel the washi tape off the wax paper using the tweezers, and carefully stick it onto the lampshade, smoothing it with your fingers to finish.

COSTUMED PUMPKINS

Have you graduated from the pumpkin-carving phase? Or have you grown tired of all orange all the time? Try this no-mess, no-fuss, lasts-all-season-long foray into pumpkin decoration!

SUPPLIES:

Real or faux pumpkins

Paintbrush

Black acrylic paint

Washi tape, in Halloween-themed patterns or colors

Scissors

Decoupage medium

1 Paint the pumpkin stems black and let them dry completely.

2 Select one washi tape pattern and, starting at the base of the stem, press a strip of tape vertically to the base of the pumpkin.

3 Repeat Step 2 on the opposite side of the pumpkin with the same tape (visually splitting the pumpkin in half).

4 Press two more lengths of tape on the opposite axis so the four pieces of tape split the pumpkin into quarters.

5 Select a second washi tape pattern and place evenly spaced strips between the four original strips. (Depending on the size of the pumpkin and the width of the tape, you may add or subtract strips of tape as desired.)

6 Trim the ends of the tape around the stem and at the base of the pumpkin. Wasn't that easy? *Optional:* Coat the pumpkin in decoupage medium to keep the strips in place.

FLUTTERY FEATHER NAPKIN RINGS

Feathers are one of those natural elements that never go out of style. These napkin rings are a cinch to make and add that fancy little touch that guests will enjoy.

SUPPLIES:

Toilet paper tube

Ruler

Floral wire

Scissors

Floral tape

Washi tape

1 Wrap the floral wire around the toilet paper tube several times to the size of the napkin ring, then cut it.

2 Slide the wire ring off the tube. Wrap floral tape around the wire, pulling it tight to activate the adhesive, until it's fully covered. Then cover with washi tape.

3 Cut a 6" piece of floral wire and fold an 8" to 10" piece of washi tape onto itself over one end of the wire.

4 Use scissors to trim the washi tape into a feather shape around the edges, with the wire acting as the shaft of the feather.

5 Cut diagonal lines into the washi tape to mimic the "vane" of a feather. Ruffle some of the pieces.

6 Repeat Steps 3 through 5 to create two or three more feathers. Add them to the napkin ring by wrapping the floral wire stem with floral tape and then with washi tape. Trim the wire as needed.

7 Repeat Steps 1 through 6 to create more napkin rings.

FRINGED PARTY BANNER

This party embellishment is ideal as a wall decoration, the background of a photo booth, or as a bunting at the base of a cake table. These are so easy to make that you can complete several of them while watching your favorite chick flick. Use wide washi tape for the biggest impact.

SUPPLIES:

Washi tape, in 3" width

Ruler

Clear tape

Baker's twine

Scissors

1 Place an 8" to 10" strip of washi tape onto your work surface, sticky side up. Use clear tape to anchor it temporarily.

2 Place the baker's twine on the washi tape, about ½" down from one of the long edges, allowing at least 12" of twine to extend from one side of the tape, for hanging.

3 Press a second strip of washi tape over the top of the first piece, sandwiching the baker's twine between them. Trim the clear tape.

4 Cut fringe into the washi tape strip, starting from the edge opposite the twine and stopping 1" from the twine (be sure not to cut through the twine).

5 Repeat Steps 1 through 4 with as many washi tape strips as you need for the desired banner length. Repeat Steps 1 through 5 to create additional banners. Hang them up using the twine that extends from either end.

SENSATIONAL SWIZZLE STICKS

Fun fact about my family: My great-grandmother had a huge collection of swizzle sticks that she kept for many years and passed down to my mother. One day they'll get passed down to me, but, in the meantime, I've started my own collection with these wood and washi tape stirrers.*

SUPPLIES:

¾" wooden circles

Washi tape, in various colors/patterns including 1 glittery roll

Ruler

Craft knife and self-healing cutting mat

Hot glue gun

Wooden coffee stirrers

1 Place 2" to 3" long strips of washi tape onto the cutting mat. Then use a craft knife to cut narrow strips about ¼" wide.

2 Press the strips onto each of the wooden circles at varying angles, overlapping them. Wrap the ends around the edges and to the back of the circles.

3 Accent each wooden circle with a strip of the glittery washi tape.

4 Hot-glue the back of each of the wooden circles to the top of a wooden stirring stick. Let cool before using.

*Note: These drink stirrers cannot be washed in the dishwasher! They are made for only a few uses.

CLASSIC PHOTO BOOTH PROPS

You spend a lot of time planning for a party, and you have everything: banners, a cake, table decor, favors . . . but it just feels like something is missing. I'm guessing you're missing a photo booth! Guests love snapping silly pics that they can instantly upload and share with friends and family. Mix these washi tape props in with scarves, hats, and more to make your party complete.

SUPPLIES:

Thick cardstock

Clip art of photo booth props*

Craft knife and self-healing cutting mat

Washi tape

Unfinished wooden dowel rods, ⅜" diameter, 1 for each prop

Hot glue gun

*Note: *Some blank props for the mustache, lips, and pipe are available to cut out from the cardstock insert between pages 150 and 151. Then skip to Step 3.*

1 Place the cardstock on the cutting mat. Lay a sheet of clip art props over it, securing the corners with tape.

2 Using the craft knife, cut out the photo booth props, making sure to cut through both layers.

3 Use washi tape to accent or completely cover the props, trimming the excess tape at the edges with the craft knife.

4 Hot-glue the props to one end of the dowel rods. Let dry and then: Say cheese!

PRETTY PLACE CARDS

Party planning isn't a skill most of us are born with, myself included. So I've had the fortune of learning about the value of place cards from a good friend who is graced with innate talent. They add a little color and touch of whimsy to any festivity—not to mention, they make guests feel warmly welcomed.

SUPPLIES:

Small tent cards

Washi tape

Scissors

Fine-tipped permanent marker,
   writing pen, or typewriter

1 Decorate each place card with washi tape in one of the following two ways:

a. Edge the top and bottom of each place card with washi tape, letting it extend halfway off the edge, then folding it over. Trim away any excess tape with scissors.

b. Tile three strips of washi tape together and cut them into a triangle. Press a triangle onto the front left of each place card, orienting it so that one of the triangle tips points to the name on the card.

2 Write or type the name of each guest on the place card. *Optional:* Use a clear label maker to write names across the cards.

SUPER STRAW FLAGS

Paper straws are very trendy, and everyone is using them at parties to serve up delicious punches and other beverages. These flags allow your guests to write their name directly on the washi tape for drink identification purposes. Not only are they just plain cute—you'll never misplace your mojito again!

SUPPLIES:

Paper straws

Ruler

Washi tape

Scissors

Pen or permanent marker (optional)

1 Tear off an approximately 5" length of washi tape and lay it adhesive side up on your work surface.

2 Place a paper straw in the center of the tape, making sure the top of the straw is about 1" to 2" past the edge of the tape.

3 Fold the tape over onto itself, catching the straw in the middle.

4 Cut a small triangle or V shape into the end of the tape flag with scissors, so that each flag ends in a dovetail shape.

5 Use a marker or pen to write a name or fun saying onto the flag for your guests, if you like!

MARVELOUS MATCHBOX FAVORS

There are all kinds of ways to give favors to your party guests, and this is yet another option. These washi-taped matchboxes are the perfect finishing touch for your celebration, and you can put all sorts of goodies inside: candies, trinkets, and more.

SUPPLIES:

Plain white matchboxes

Washi tape, in standard width and narrow width

Craft knife and self-healing cutting mat

1 Tear off two pieces of the standard-width washi tape and arrange them on the top of one of the matchboxes so they meet in a V at the center.

2 Use the craft knife to cut a mitered corner where the two pieces of washi tape meet (see page 13).

3 Tear off two pieces of the narrow washi tape and arrange them in an X, aligning them at the end of the washi tape V.

4 Trim any excess washi tape at the edges with the craft knife.

5 Repeat Steps 1 through 4 on the remaining matchboxes.

TRY THIS NEXT:
Make multiple Xs to expand the pattern or replace the geometry with another design entirely—think flowers, trees, or birds!

MODERN MENORAH

If you celebrate Hanukkah, here's an opportunity to make an extra special menorah for the festival of lights. This modern take on the most important symbol of the winter-time holiday uses wooden blocks to create a clean and elegant look that's totally customizable. To make your nightly candle lighting even prettier, try finding candles that match the color scheme of your menorah!

SUPPLIES:

9 wooden 2" × 2" blocks

9 wooden candle cups

Paintbrushes

Acrylic paint, in white and silver

Craft glue

9 candles that fit the candle cups

Washi tape, in silver and 2 other colors of your choice, in standard and thin widths

Wax paper

Pencil

Craft knife and self-healing cutting mat

Decoupage medium

1 Paint eight of the wooden blocks white and the remaining block plus all of the candle cups silver. Give them several coats, then let dry.

2 Glue one candle cup to the top of each wooden block, then let them dry.

3 Wrap one strip of silver washi tape around each of the white blocks, about $3/8$" from the top edge, overlapping the ends about $1/4$" at the back.

4 Wrap a thinner-width tape around each of the white blocks about $1/8$" above the silver tape.

5 Wrap a standard-width tape around the white blocks about ¼" below the silver tape.

6 Place a piece of wax paper on the cutting mat. Tile together three strips of standard-width tape, overlapping them slightly, on the wax paper. Flip the sheet over and draw or trace a six-pointed star, about ½" in diameter, on the back. Then cut it out through both layers (wax paper and washi tape).

7 Peel the washi tape "sticker" off the wax paper. Center and press it onto one side of the silver block. Wrap a strip of coordinating washi tape around the base of the candle cup on the silver block.

8 Paint decoupage medium over the candleholders to seal the washi tape.

9 Place a candle into each of the holders. Line up the wooden blocks with the silver one (containing the shammes candle, the one used for lighting) in the center.

TRY THIS NEXT:
Switch the stripes from horizontal to vertical or, keep them horizontal and vary the placement on each block so that the outermost holders have the stripe on the very bottom edge and the innermost have it at the top—it will look like steps leading right up to the shammes candle.

2-D CHRISTMAS TREE

Who doesn't love-love-love a good Christmas tree? There's something pleasing about the simple shape, the woody smell—and the tradition of decorating it. If you travel during the holidays, though, you know that having a real one that requires regular watering is impractical. With a washi tape tree, you sacrifice that fresh-cut smell, but there's no risk of it drying up—and your cats won't try to climb it! Oh, and the cleanup is quick and painless—no pine needles!

SUPPLIES:

Wall space, about 4' × 6'

Washi tape, 2 rolls in wood grain, 2 rolls in shades of green, 1 roll in red, at least 1 roll in shades of gold

Flat wooden or cardboard circle shapes, 3½" and 4¼" in diameter

Flat wooden or cardboard star shape, 8" diameter

Measuring tape

Pencil

Scissors

Temporary wall adhesive

1 Press a 4' strip of wood-grain washi tape so that it extends vertically up the wall from the floor.

2 Add two strips on either side of the first strip, so the trunk of the tree is a total of five strips wide. Taper the trunk at the top, using scissors to cut the ends. Cut the strips directly to the left and right of the center ½" shorter than the center one, and the next two strips ½" shorter than those.

3 Measure and mark about 7" up from the bottom of the trunk.

4 Using the mark as a guide, press a 21" strip of green washi tape that extends perpendicularly on one side of the trunk. Repeat on the opposite side of the trunk to begin the first pair of branches.

5 Add two more strips of green tape on top of each branch, each 20" and 19" respectively, to thicken it.

6 Measure and mark 6" up the trunk from the top of each branch.

7 Repeat Steps 4, 5, and 6 for the remaining six pairs of branches, subtracting 1" for each strip of tape. (The washi tape strips that make up the last pair of branches should be 3", 2", and 1" long.)

8 Wrap the star with strips of gold washi tape, and wrap the remaining shapes in red.

9 Attach temporary adhesive to the backs of the shapes, and press them onto the tree—adding the star at the very top!

TRY THIS NEXT:
If you're open to making holes in the wall, insert tacks over the tree branches. Then hang three-dimensional ornaments or Advent envelopes (see page 245) from them.

ADVENT CALENDAR MOBILE

Confession: Advent calendars are one of my true craft obsessions. (I once made a huge version on a canvas with 25 papier-mâché boxes. It was colorful and, quite frankly, amazing.) Here's a Calder-inspired washi tape version that may be my favorite yet.

SUPPLIES:

2 embroidery hoops, in 8" and 10" diameters

Spray paint

Tape measure

Pencil

Ruler

Roll of kraft paper

Scissors

Permanent marker

Number stencils

Washi tape

Hole punch

Small drill

25 small treats*

Clear jewelry floss

Hot glue gun (optional)

Baker's twine, about 20'

Large-holed needle

*Note: *The gifts can't be too heavy or large, but there are plenty of treats that are small and lightweight enough (stickers, temporary tattoos, small candies) to fit into the hanging envelopes!*

1 Separate the inner rings from the outer rings of the embroidery hoops. (You are just going to use the inner rings.)

2 Spray-paint both rings. Let them dry, flip them over, and repeat until

the rings are fully covered. Set them aside to dry completely.

3 Measure and mark fifty 2" × 3" rectangles onto the kraft paper. Cut them out.

4 Use the marker and number stencils to mark the numbers 1 through 25 on 25 of the kraft paper rectangles.

5 Place a numbered rectangle on top of a blank rectangle and align the edges.

6 Press a strip of washi tape on each of three edges of the rectangle (left, right, and bottom), allowing half of the strip to extend over the edge.

7 Fold the washi tape around to the back of the rectangle, securing the two layers of kraft paper together. Trim the corners with scissors as needed.

8 Repeat Steps 5 through 7 until all 25 envelopes are complete.

9 Punch a hole at the top of each envelope, about ½" from the untaped edge. Fill each one with a small treat, then set aside.

10 Measure and mark 3 evenly spaced dots around the outside of each of the two inner hoops. Drill a small hole at each dot. (You will use these holes to string the rings together and to hang the mobile—mark them so that you will be able to distinguish them from holes you will drill in future steps.)

11 Mark 13 additional dots around the outside of the larger hoop. Measure and mark 12 dots around the outside of the smaller hoop. Drill a hole at each dot. (You will use these holes to string the envelopes to the mobile.)

12 To assemble the mobile, place the smaller hoop inside the larger hoop, then tie an 8" strand of clear jewelry floss to connect a hanging hole on one hoop to the corresponding hole on the other hoop, knotting to tie it off. *Optional:* Place a small dab of hot glue onto each knot to secure it.

13 Repeat Step 12 with the two remaining pairs of the three hanging holes. When finished, the smaller hoop should dangle below the larger hoop.

14 Thread a 12" strand of clear jewelry floss through each of the same three hanging holes in the large hoop and knot them there. Then knot the strands together at the top. (This will be the way you hang the mobile.)

15 Once the mobile base is assembled, use the baker's twine to hang packages from the 13 holes drilled in the large hoop and the 12 holes drilled in the small hoop. Tie one end of the baker's twine into a bow through the punched hole in the envelope, and use the needle to thread the other end through a hole in one of the hoops and tie it.

16 Each day in December, pull the thread hanging from an envelope to release the bow, remove the gift package from the mobile, and peek inside!

HOLIDAY GIFT STATIONERY SET

Did you get pulled into an office Secret Santa gift exchange? Giving gifts is fun, but it can be stressful if you aren't exactly sure what to get your coworker. Stationery is my go-to, since it's customizable for all ages, male or female—and you can personalize with the recipient's initials.

SUPPLIES:

Plain white cardstock, 8½" × 5½" (half the size of a regular sheet of letter paper)

Washi tape, in metallic shades or patterns

Ruler

Scissors

Rubber stamp letter set or stamp with a personalized image or greeting

Ink pad that coordinates with the washi tape

White envelopes (4¼" × 6¼") that fit the white paper

Baker's twine

1 Press a piece of washi tape about 1" in along a short side of a piece of cardstock. Trim the edges.

2 Choose a stamp, place it on the ink pad, stamp it onto the paper above the washi tape line, and let dry.

3 Decorate the top front or back of an envelope with a strip of washi tape to coordinate with the piece of cardstock.

4 Repeat Steps 1 through 3, decorating at least 10 sheets of cardstock and 10 envelopes to make a complete set.

5 Once the set is complete, stack them and tie together with baker's twine before giving the set as a gift.

JOLLY HOLIDAY ORNAMENTS

You never walk into the craft shop *needing* flat holiday ornaments, but they're the sort of things that end up hopping into the basket anyway. Luckily, they're also the sort of things that can be enough of an inspiring blank canvas they will actually get made (rather than stashed in a drawer). This is a quick and easy way to add a special set of ornaments to your collection.

SUPPLIES:

Flat, clear acrylic plastic or glass ornaments, with a hole at the top

Paintbrush

Acrylic paint, in white

Washi tape, 3 to 6 rolls in holiday patterns and in varying widths

Scissors

Craft knife and self-healing cutting mat

Pencil

Baker's twine, 8" to 12" per ornament

1 Paint the back of each ornament with white acrylic paint until fully coated. Let them dry.

2 Using two or three rolls of tape per ornament, press strips of washi tape over the top of the ornament, working horizontally, vertically, or diagonally.

3 When the ornament is covered to your satisfaction, flip it facedown onto your cutting mat and trim around the edges with the craft knife. Poke through the hole with the tip of a pencil, and press the edges inside the hole.

4 Thread the baker's twine through the hole in the top of the ornament and tie the ends together.

YULETIDE CANDLES

The days get short and dark come holiday season, and candles offer a sweet glow—not to mention a variety of scents (like gingerbread and evergreen)—to help dial up the cozy factor. I'm not a big fan of the labels that come on candles, and I'm bored by plain pillars, so . . . washi tape! And the added bonus? If you need a last-minute hostess gift, just pop one of these pretties in a bag.

SUPPLIES:

Large wax candles

Washi tape, in festive colors or patterns

Scissors

1 Cut the washi tape into long strips.

2 Wrap the strips in different ways onto your candles:

a. in vertical stripes, starting at the top and running the length of the candle, trimming the tape at the bottom

b. in diagonal stripes, to create a spiral effect

c. in horizontal stripes, around the candle, making sure that the washi tape ends overlap at the back and stick to each other

3 Trim the ends of the tape at the top and bottom edges of the candles.

Note: *As the candle burns, trim the washi tape at the top edge. And, for safety, never leave an open flame unattended.*

MINI PALLET COASTERS

This project turns regular craft sticks into small replicas of wooden pallets. Once they're embellished with patterned washi tape, they become the cutest DIY coasters ever! They're perfect for gifts, but it's completely understandable if you simply have to keep them for yourself instead.

SUPPLIES:

42 wooden craft sticks
  (to make 6 coasters)

½" square balsa wood rod

Pencil

Ruler

Pliers with wire-cutting blade

Craft knife and self-healing cutting mat

Sandpaper

Washi tape

Scissors

Hot glue gun

Decoupage medium, in matte finish

Paintbrush

1 Measure and mark seven 4" segments along the wooden craft sticks and three 4" segments along the balsa wood rod.

2 Using the wire-cutting blade on the pliers, snip off the ends of each craft stick. Use the craft knife to cut through the balsa wood rod (the balsa wood is very soft—to create a full cut all the way through, just press down the blade on all four sides).

3 Sand any rough edges using a sheet of sandpaper.

4 Cut 42 strips of washi tape and press each strip along one side of a craft stick. Use sharp scissors to trim the ends of the tape flush with the end of each craft stick. Wrap the edges of the washi tape around the sides of each craft stick.

5 Line up the 3 balsa wood sections, spaced evenly apart, and hot-glue one washi tape stick on the top and one on the bottom.

6 Hot-glue a stick centered across the middle. Add the remaining craft sticks, evenly spacing them and arranging them according to the reference diagram.

7 Apply one coat of decoupage medium over the top of the coasters to seal the tape. Let them dry completely before using.

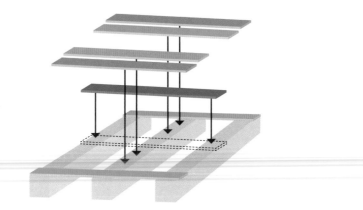

CHAPTER 6

JUST FOR FUN

WOODEN MATCHING GAME

This DIY memory game will keep kids busy for hours. Bonus: When your little one loses a game piece, simply make another! Just remember to use the same pattern of washi tape on the back.

SUPPLIES:

24 wooden circles, 2" diameter

Washi tape, in 2 to 12 colors

Scissors or a craft knife

Paintbrush

Wax paper

Punches in various shapes,
    at least 12 (or a craft knife and
    self-healing cutting mat)

Decoupage medium, in matte finish

1 Press strips of the same color tape across one side of each of the circles, covering them completely.

2 Flip the circles over and trim the excess washi tape around the edges.

3 Tile strips of washi tape together on the wax paper (overlapping each strip about ⅛").

4 Use the paper punches to punch out two of each shape. Or, double over the wax paper and cut two matching shapes at once using the craft knife. *Note:* For this to work, they must be shapes that are symmetrical left to right.

5 Peel up each shape and stick it to the front of one of the wooden circles.

6 Paint a layer of decoupage medium over the front of each wooden circle. Let dry completely, then paint the back. Let dry, again, before using.

WASHI TAPE ID SYSTEM

As easy as washi tape is, there is one thing that can be a struggle: keeping track of it all. Because, let's be honest, once you get one roll, you're on your way to getting 50. Make this simple ID system to keep track of the patterns and colors you have in your stash and, more important, to see how they look off the roll.

SUPPLIES:

Extra-large cardstock gift tags

Washi tape, every roll in your collection

2" storage rings

1 Tear a 1" to 2" piece of washi tape from every roll you have. Make sure, if it's a patterned tape, that there is a long enough piece to display a full cycle of the pattern.

2 Press each piece onto a cardstock gift tag.

3 On the back of each tag write any valuable notes about the tape, like where you purchased it, and when.

4 String the tags onto the storage ring, and clip it closed.

WASHI TAPE DOWEL DISPLAY

There are so many great ways to store washi tape, and this dowel version is a classic. What you are looking for in any good holder is an easy way to tear washi off the roll, and an easy way to add new rolls and remove empty ones. This organizer fits the bill.

SUPPLIES:

14" wooden dowl rod, ½" in diameter

Sandpaper

2 eye screws

Ribbon, twine, or string

Washi tape

Craft knife

Nail or picture hook

1 Sand the cut ends of the dowel. Then screw one of the eye screws into each end.

2 Double-knot one end of the ribbon through the eye of one screw.

3 Press strips of washi tape lengthwise along the dowel, covering it, trimming the tape at each end.

4 Slide the dowel through the center of the washi tape rolls, making sure that the rolls are oriented in the same direction.

5 Tie the loose end of the ribbon to the other end of the dowel using a slip knot, so that it's easier to open and remove tape rolls if necessary.

6 Hang the dowel on the wall using a nail or picture hook.

TRY THIS NEXT:
For another washi tape storage option that is meant to be seen, turn to page 269.

DECORATED KEYBOARD

This is the kind of washi tape project that turns heads. You'll be typing away at your desk, the coffee shop, wherever—and, inevitably, someone will ask, "Where can I get one?"

SUPPLIES:

Computer keyboard

Ruler

Washi tape, in 3 to 4 rolls, in complementary colors

Scissors

1 Unplug and disconnect your keyboard before starting this project.

2 Measure the keys on your keyboard, starting with the main letter keys, and moving to the larger and smaller function keys such as the space bar, tab, shift, and so on.

3 Cut squares and rectangles from several different colors of washi tape to fit all of the keys. Press the appropriate shape onto each key.

4 Smooth the shapes completely before turning on and plugging in again.

7 week 29

13
MON

14
TUE

15
WED

16
THU

COLOR-CODED DAY PLANNER

It can be really difficult to keep track of *where* you've written something in a notebook or planner full of notes. Here's the perfect solution: Divide a planner into sections using a color-coded system on the edges of the pages. With a quick glance, you'll know right where you need to be.

SUPPLIES:

Planner or notebook

Washi tape, in at least 12 colors

Scissors

1 Divide the planner into sections however you like (12 months, 52 weeks, and so forth)—you'll use one washi tape color per section.

2 Tear off a length of washi tape that's slightly longer than the height of the pages in the planner.

3 Press just half of the strip of washi tape vertically along the right side of one page, leaving the other half hanging off the edge.

4 Fold the remaining half over the edge of the page and press. Then trim the edges at the top and bottom with scissors.

5 Repeat Steps 2 through 4 with the same color washi tape for all pages of the same category.

6 Repeat Steps 2 through 5 on the next section with a different color washi tape. Continue switching tape color or pattern with each new section. Place tape until the edges are all color coded.

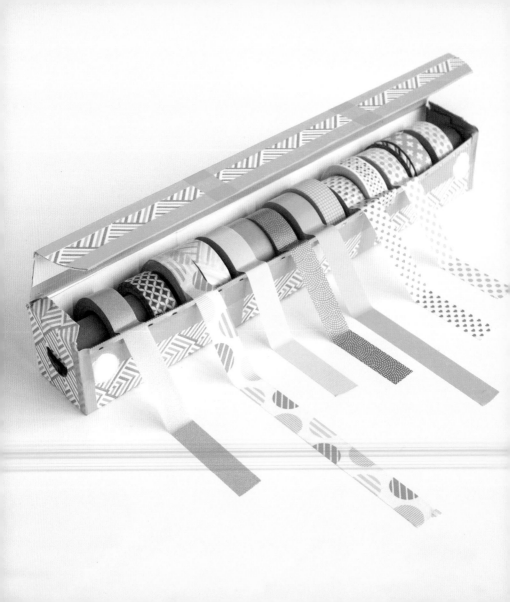

WASHI TAPE DISPENSER

My washi tape collection was previously not organized at all. I'd have to dig out a tape roll from a large drawer and then fumble with it to find the end of the tape. This dispenser solves both of those problems. You can store your washi and easily tear off a piece—oh, and the storage looks great on a desktop.

SUPPLIES:

An empty plastic wrap or aluminum foil box and tube

Paintbrushes

Acrylic paint

Washi tape

Scissors

Decoupage medium

Adhesive Velcro dots

1 Paint the entire box, inside and out. Let it dry.

2 Press strips of washi tape vertically or horizontally across the outside of the box, covering it completely.

3 Use scissors to trim the ends of the tape at the edges of the box.

4 Paint two coats of decoupage medium over the box, then let it dry.

5 Apply three evenly spaced adhesive Velcro dots across the inside of the box flap, with their matches aligned below the serrated edge to close the box.

6 Slide the washi tape rolls onto the empty tube and store them inside the box. Pull the washi tape out and fold it over the serrated lip, so you can trim the tape as you dispense it.

EASY BREEZY BICYCLE

Let's be honest: If you complete this project, you're going to be the envy of all your friends. Dazzle up a new bicycle, or revamp a thrift store find. Add a sealant over the top to make the washi tape decoration permanent, or allow it to be temporary—remove it when inclement weather blows in. *Note:* This project is relatively easy but requires a significant time commitment!

SUPPLIES:

Washi tape, in 3 to 4 complementary colors

Cruiser bike

Flexible tape measure

Scissors

Glue (optional)

Decoupage medium, or a weatherproof sealant if you want your decorations to be permanent (optional)

Paintbrush (optional)

1 Measure the circumference of all the bars on the bicycle. Add $\frac{1}{2}$" to all measurements.

2 Cut strips of washi tape equal in length to the measurements determined in Step 1.

3 Wrap a washi tape strip around one bicycle bar, overlapping the ends so it sticks to itself. Use a dab of glue, if needed, to reinforce the overlap (just make sure to avoid getting glue on the bicycle if you want the tape to be temporary).

4 Repeat Step 3, adding strips of different colors (randomly or in a repeating pattern) to all bicycle bars until the entire bicycle is decorated. *Optional:* Apply a sealant to weatherproof the bike surface.

BONNY BUSINESS CARDS

People go to great lengths to make a first impression, and a well-designed business card can help. Handmade ones are typically the most winning. So here's your opportunity to make a lasting impact that will have people saying, "She's cool, she's creative—let's work together!"

SUPPLIES:

Business card blanks, in ivory

Computer with word-processing or design program and printer

Heavy-duty craft knife and self-healing cutting mat

Ruler

Chipboard

Glue dots or double-sided tape

Washi tape

1 Using a word-processing program or design app, determine what you want your business cards to say and how you want them to look. Then print your design onto the card blanks, and let the ink dry.

2 While the ink is drying, use your heavy-duty craft knife to cut a 2¼" × 3¾" chipboard rectangle for each business card.

3 Place one business card in the center of a chipboard rectangle, and adhere with a few glue dots or double-sided tape.

4 Tear some washi tape off of the roll and press it onto the corners of the business card.

FANCY BANDAGES FOR BOO-BOOS

Decorated bandages are simple to make and bring a smile when it's needed most. And, oddly enough, they make wounds heal more quickly. I promise!

SUPPLIES:

Adhesive bandages

Washi tape

Scissors

Plastic zip-top bag

1 Remove the outer packaging from the bandage (keep the backing on the adhesive strips in place).

2 Press the washi tape down the length of the bandage and smooth it.

3 Use scissors to trim any excess washi tape around the edges.

4 Store in a plastic zip-top bag until you need to use.

FOLD-UP PLAY MAT

My brothers adored playing on their city-themed play mat when they were younger. Their mat was actually a rug, though, so it was a bear to bring out, heavy, and required a lot of room to store. This version is less expensive, lightweight, and easy to fold up and stow in downtimes.

SUPPLIES:

Tri-fold project board

Washi tape

Ruler or straightedge

Scissors

Toilet paper roll (optional)

1 Open the project board and lay it flat on the work surface.

2 Find the approximate center, and press down four pieces of washi tape to make a rectangle (could be a building or a village green).

3 Working your way out toward the edges, press down strips of washi tape to outline roads (make sure the width of each road is about 3" wide,

to fit two lanes for standard-size Matchbox cars).

4 Cut small rectangles of narrow-width washi tape, then apply them down the center of the roads as dashed lines.

5 Populate the city with different-sized buildings, parking spaces, and even a roundabout! *Optional:* Add temporary tunnels out of washi-taped toilet paper tubes.

6 Fold the board flat and place it under a bed or in a closet when not in use.

SNAPPY CELL PHONE COVER

Have you seen the prices of cell phone cases? Some of them are outrageous! Instead of spending your inheritance to protect your phone, buy a basic clear or white case and decorate it with washi tape. It will look just as good as—nay, *better than*—any other version but will cost a fraction of the price.

SUPPLIES:

Blank cell phone case

Washi tape, in narrow width,
  in 2 to 3 coordinating colors

Craft knife and self-healing cutting mat

Paintbrush

Decoupage medium

1 Starting from the bottom of the case, press 5 or 6 strips of one washi tape color, angling them slightly so they cross and overlap.

2 Wrap the ends of the tape around the edges of the case and trim off the excess tape with a craft knife.

3 Repeat Steps 1 and 2 with each color of washi tape until the back of the case is entirely covered.

4 Flip the case onto your cutting mat, washi tape side down. Cut around the edge of the camera hole with the craft knife to remove the washi tape.

5 Paint decoupage medium over the outside of the case to seal the washi tape. Let dry for 24 hours before inserting a phone.

WESTPORT, CT

WWW.SHOPTERRAIN.COM

★ CALIFORNIA ★

CALIFORNIA
1

SPIFFY REUSABLE STRIPS

Washi tape is, by nature, temporary. But by combining these properties with a product like Scotch Restickable Strips, you can extend the life of your favorite tape design indefinitely. With reusable washi tape strips, you can, say, switch out your kid's art or your friend's vacation postcards on the fridge without blowing through your supply of washi tape. Another benefit: The reusable strips maintain the translucent nature of washi tape that everyone knows and loves!

SUPPLIES:

Scotch Restickable Strips, in 1" × 3" size
Washi tape, standard width
Craft knife and self-healing cutting mat

1 Peel off one of the reusable adhesive strips, keeping the plastic protective sheet attached to the back. Lay it flat on your cutting mat, sticky side up (plastic sheet down).

2 Press two strips of washi tape next to each other on the adhesive strip.

3 Cut the adhesive strip lengthwise down the middle (so it's now the approximate width of a piece of washi tape) and trim off any excess washi tape around the edges.

4 Cut the ends of each strip with the craft knife to resemble the torn edges of washi tape.

5 Repeat Steps 1 through 4 on the remaining five adhesive strips in the package. Then use them to stick up your favorite artwork!

KEY IDENTIFICATION

Why is it that whenever I am searching for the right key to fit a particular lock, it's always the last one I try? I've seen those plastic keyholders at various stores, but I don't want anything that makes my key ring bulkier (I carry enough already!). So I came up with a simple (washi tape) solution. With washi tape and some clear nail polish, you'll never be wondering which is the right key again.

SUPPLIES:

Keys

Washi tape, in as many colors/patterns as you have keys

Craft knife and self-healing cutting mat

Clear nail polish

1 Press 2 strips of washi tape across one side of the head of a key, overlapping them about ⅛".

2 Flip the key over onto your cutting mat, then trace the outside edge of the key head with the craft knife to cut off the excess tape.

3 Using the same color tape, repeat Steps 1 and 2 to apply tape to the opposite side of the key.

4 Repeat Steps 1 through 3, using a different color tape for each key.

5 Paint at least 2 coats of clear nail polish on one side of all of the keys to seal the tape. Let them dry completely. Then flip them over to coat the opposite side of each key. Let dry completely before using.

TINY TIN STORAGE

If you regularly purchase tins of mints (or other tiny edibles), start saving the containers. Because if you decorate one with washi tape, it can be transformed into any number of things: business card holder, sewing kit, small craft supply storage, mini first aid kit, travel jewelry case . . . or candy dispenser!

SUPPLIES:

Metal mint containers (ideally with flat tops free of any raised writing)

Spray primer

Washi tape

Scissors

Craft knife

Paintbrush

Decoupage medium

1 In a well-ventilated space, spray a base coat of primer over the lid of each tin. *Tip:* For an even finish, spray several light coats with a lot of drying time in between. Let dry completely.

2 Press strips of washi tape across the cover of each tin, and wrap the tape down the sides. Snip the tape at the corners, so you can dart them and fold down the pieces smoothly.

3 Use the craft knife to trace the edge of each lid, just above the lip, to trim the excess tape at the edges.

4 Paint a coat of decoupage medium over the top of each tin to seal the washi tape. Let them dry completely before filling the tins.

SEWING TAPE MEASURE

I don't know a single crafty person who doesn't love receiving fun notions as gifts. This washi'd tape measure is a tribute to all the sewists out there. Give this as a gift to your favorite seamstress.

SUPPLIES:

Retractable soft tape measure

Washi tape

Craft knife and self-healing cutting mat

① Press strips of washi tape side by side onto one side of the tape measure housing.

② Flip the tape measure washi side down onto the cutting mat, then trace around the edge of the housing with the craft knife to cut off the excess washi tape at the edges.

③ Repeat Steps 1 and 2 on the opposite side of the tape measure housing.

④ Use the craft knife to trim around the retraction button, so the button can move freely.

TRY THIS NEXT:
Press strips of tape onto wax paper and use a ¼" standard hole punch to cut dots from the tape. Peel them off the wax paper backing, and place polka dots over the first layer of washi tape!

NUMBER FLASH CARDS

Flash cards are a proven memory tool and study aid. Start kids early with a handmade washi-taped set. They'll be encouraged to learn their numbers (or colors, states and capitals, vocabulary, and so on) in no time.

SUPPLIES:

Printer paper, in at least 32-lb weight

Computer with access to the Internet (or a word-processing program) and a printer

Online flash card generator

Paper cutter

Washi tape

Scissors

1 Use an online flash card generator to create the flash cards. (Alternatively, divide a document page into quarters and type up your own flash cards.)

2 Print the cards onto sturdy paper, then use a paper cutter (or scissors) to trim them to size.

3 Press strips of washi tape along the sides of each card, applying it so that half of the width of the tape extends off the edge. Fold the excess tape to the back of the cards, and trim (or miter, see page 13) any excess tape at the corners.

TRY THIS NEXT:
Cut or punch shapes from washi tape in different colors to make flash cards that test shapes or colors, respectively.

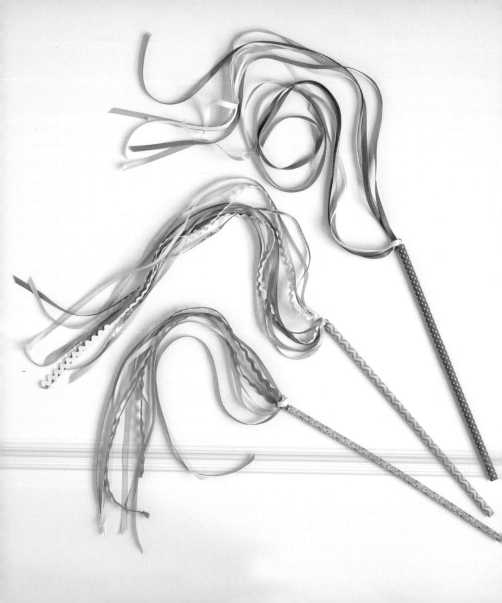

WHIMSICAL RIBBON WAND

If you know a child who's fascinated by wands, chances are he or she has already worn out a couple of them. Instead of purchasing a new one, create your own with a dowel rod and ribbon—and washi tape. You'll be surprised at how well it holds up!

SUPPLIES:

12" wooden dowel rod, ⅜" in diameter

Washi tape, in wide or standard width

Scissors

Eye screw

Ribbon, in 6 different colors

Measuring tape or ruler

1 Cut a length of washi tape slightly longer than your dowel.

2 Lay it down on your work surface, adhesive side up, and center and press the wand onto it lengthwise. Wrap the edges of the tape around the wand. If you use wide tape, this is the only piece you'll need.

3 Repeat Steps 1 and 2 to add a second piece of tape on the opposite side of the dowel to cover it, if needed.

4 Cut the excess tape flush with each end of the dowel.

5 Screw the eye screw into one end of the dowel, leaving it to extend about ½" off the end.

6 Cut 6 pieces of 32" lengths of ribbon.

7 Gather and tie the ends of the ribbons in a single tight knot around the eye screw.

CRAFTY STICK FRAME

Popsicle sticks practically scream "kid crafts" to most people, but there are more sophisticated applications for them, and this is one. Once they're assembled into a frame, glue magnets or a picture hanger to the back and you can proudly display your project with the utmost conviction—no one will think you made it at summer camp!

SUPPLIES:

12 large wooden craft sticks (tongue depressors)

Washi tape

Craft knife and self-healing cutting mat

Hot glue gun

Photos

Glue dots or double-stick tape

1 Roll out a strip of washi tape about 2" longer than the craft sticks, keeping the adhesive side up.

2 Press a craft stick onto the adhesive side of the washi tape, then wrap or trim the excess tape around the edges.

3 Repeat Steps 1 and 2 until you have covered 10 sticks.

4 Line up the sticks vertically, washi tape side down, one right next to the other.

5 Hot-glue the two remaining sticks horizontally across the back of the sticks to secure them in place.

6 Flip the frame over and use glue dots or double-stick tape to adhere your photo(s) to the front.

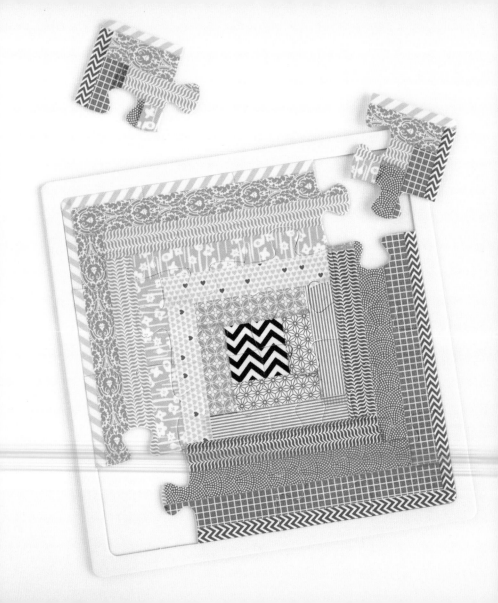

PATCHWORK PUZZLE

When I was four years old, my mother gave me a photo puzzle of a goat. I treasured that gift for years, and I still enjoy puzzles to this day. If you want a great present for a child that will start him or her on a lifetime of loving puzzles, this washi tape version is a perfect bet.

SUPPLIES:

Wooden or cardboard puzzle blank

Paintbrushes

Acrylic paint, in white

Washi tape, in 12 coordinating colors/
  patterns

Ruler

Scissors

Craft knife and self-healing cutting mat

Decoupage medium

1 Separate the pieces of the puzzle blank. Then paint each of the pieces white. Let them dry.

2 Reassemble the puzzle. Center and press a 1¼" square of tape onto the puzzle.

3 Select two more colors and press strips around the center square so they frame it. Trim the corners so they overlap or abut (see pages 14–15).

4 Repeat Step 3 as many times as needed to fill the entire puzzle surface.

5 Flip the taped puzzle pieces onto the cutting mat, and use the craft knife to cut along the puzzle piece edges to separate them.

6 Paint a coat of decoupage medium over the top of each piece to seal the tape. Let them dry, then move the puzzle pieces back into the base.

CITY SKYLINE TABLET CASE MAKEOVER

Avoid an instance of mistaken identity by personalizing your tablet case with—what else?—washi tape, of course! This project is similar to the Snappy Cell Phone Cover (see page 279) but with a more structured design that, once you've mastered, you can apply to any surface.

SUPPLIES:

Plastic case to fit your electronic tablet

Ruler

Washi tape, in 3 to 5 coordinating colors/patterns

Wax paper

Craft knife and self-healing cutting mat

Paintbrush

Decoupage medium

1 Apply two 8" to 10" strips of washi tape from one roll onto a sheet of wax paper, overlapping them about ⅛". Repeat with two strips from the second roll of tape, and so on, until you've created a sheet of washi tape strips about equal to the width of the case.

2 Orient the wax paper so that the strips run vertically, and place on the cutting mat. With a craft knife, cut the tops of the strips of washi tape at varying angles to mimic the rooftops of buildings (customize for a particular city's skyline).

3 Peel the sheet of buildings off the wax paper, and align and press down the bottom of the buildings onto the bottom of the case. *Optional:* Cut a circle or crescent shape to add a moon or sun to the sky.

4 Press a strip of washi tape across the bottom of the case (overlapping the base of each building) to secure the bottom edges of the strips.

5 Paint a layer of decoupage medium across the back of the entire case to seal the washi tape. Let it dry completely before attaching it to your tablet.

TRY THIS NEXT:
Enlarge the proportions of the skyline design to fit a bedroom wall, and you'll have your very own room with a view!

RESOURCES

HOW TO ORGANIZE YOUR WASHI TAPE

Now that you have a boatload of washi tape, how do you organize it? This task is actually one of the best parts of owning washi tape! Here are some of my favorite ideas for displaying washi:

Upcycled aluminum foil box *(see Washi Tape Dispenser, page 269)*

Dowel hung with ribbon *(see Washi Tape Dowel Display, page 263)*

Thread spool rack

Large glass jar

Old wooden floor grate *(rolls of standard-width washi tape fit perfectly into the spaces between the gratings)*

Wooden cassette tape rack

Pegboard with hooks

Dress pants holder *(slide rolls of washi tape onto the removable dowel)*

Metal hanger *(snip open one side of the hanger, in order to slide rolls of washi tape onto the straight base wire)*

Coffee capsule holder

Command hooks and dowel rods

And I'm sure there are so many more! Send pictures of your ingenious washi tape organization systems to amy@washitapecrafts.com—or post them with #washitapecrafts.

WASHI TAPE INSPIRATION

There are several online sites and blogs that are devoted to providing the "best of" washi tape tutorials and inspiration. Here are some of my favorites:

Washi Tape Crafts (my blog!): *washitapecrafts.com*

Cute Tape: *cutetape.com/creative/creations*

Omiyage: *omiyage.ca*

The Washi Blog: *thewashiblog.com*

Washi Tape Ideas: *washitapeideas.com*

PURCHASING WASHI TAPE

The original brand of washi tape is MT, a Japanese company. Since it was launched, several large companies have jumped on the washi bandwagon, including Duck brand and Scotch. If you're on the search for great patterns and colors, here are some of my favorite sources to shop.

amazon.com	**michaels.com**
consumercrafts.com	**officedepot.com**
cutetape.com	**omiyage.ca**
etsy.com	**simonsaysstamp.com**
ginkopapers.com	**stampington.com**
happytape.bigcartel.com	**staples.com**
joann.com	**wishywashi.com**

SURFACES AND SUPPLIES USED IN THIS BOOK

Listed in order by project, here is the sourcing information for many of the specialty items used in making the projects in this book.

5-Minute Garden Markers, page 49: *The blank "6-inch wooden plant labels" are from homedepot.com.*

Quick-and-Easy Gift Tags, page 61: *Avery brand makes blank white tags, available at stationery and office supply stores, and online retailers like amazon.com and staples.com.*

Statement Ceiling Fan, page 73: *The ceiling fan used in these pages was purchased at Lowe's.*

Insta-Wall Art, page 113: *The projects in this book were made using four 4" × 4" Artist's Loft brand back-stapled deco canvas, available at michaels.com and many other craft retailers.*

Sweet Spice Jars, page 119: *The glass spice jars with clips that are featured in this book were sourced from crateandbarrel.com (as a set of 12), but similar options are also available at stores/sites like containerstore.com.*

Photo-Transfer Pillow, page 121: *The white cotton pillow cover featured in this book was from muji.com.*

Cheery Chair Upgrade, page 123: *The chairs featured in this book were made using the Boraam Industried Windsor Dining Chair Set of 2, from target.com.*

Woven-Top End Table, page 125: *The table in this book was made using the Ikea Lack table from ikea.com.*

Bold Bangle Bracelets, page 149: *These wooden bangle bracelets are ReadyToDecorate brand, purchased from amazon.com.*

Make It Modern Pendant, page 167: *The pendant backer ("1-inch round pendant trays") and the clear insert ("round glass domed cabochon") are both CleverDelights brand, and both were purchased from amazon.com.*

Glamour Rings, page 171: *The ring blanks are Find-Its brand, purchased from amazon.com.*

Party Mask, page 215: *The base for this project is the "white paper half mask" offered by Creatology brand, purchased from michaels.com.*

Jack-o'-Lamp, page 221: *The lamp used in this book is the Lykta lamp from ikea.com.*

Pretty Place Cards, page 233: *Blank tent cards are Avery brand, purchased from target.com.*

Marvelous Matchbox Favors, page 237: *For blank matchboxes, look for "plain white cover wooden matches," available via amazon.com.*

Modern Menorah, page 239: *The wooden blocks and candle cups were sourced from michaels.com.*

Washi Tape ID System, page 261: *2"-diameter metal hinging rings are available from edupress.com, as "Flashcard Sort and Store Rings."*

Easy Breezy Bicycle, page 271: *The model used in this book is the Schwinn Womens Legacy 26" Cruiser Bike in blue and white, from target.com.*

Sewing Tape Measure, page 287: *Retractable 60" tape measure sourced from staples.com.*

Number Flash Cards, page 289: *Search online for "flash card generator" or "printable flash cards" (example: aplusmath.com/flashcards/Flashcard_Creator.html).*

City Skyline Tablet Case Makeover, page 297: *The case used for the project shown in this book is part (just used the back case) of the Besdata brand "Ultra Thin Magnetic Smart Cover and Back Case for Apple iPad" in white.*

RECOMMENDED SUPPLIES

One of washi tape's greatest assets—it's temporary!—becomes its greatest deficit after you've created that great washi tape masterpiece that you want to hold up in the shower (I exaggerate, but still . . .). The point is, coating washi tape in some sort of sealant, whether it's a decoupage medium, a spray sealant, or a pour-on sealant, will make it last longer.

Mod Podge: *I'm partial to all Mod Podge products when it comes to seeking out the perfect decoupage medium (full disclosure, I also founded and host the ModPodgeRocks.com blog, so there's a lot of love there).*

Dimensional Magic: *Dimensional Magic is an acrylic resin-like product used to add raised embellishments to surfaces—such as those in projects like the Bohemian Belt Buckle (page 151). It dries clear and allows the full color of the surface below to show through.*

Minwax Polycrylic Protective Finish: *This spray-on or brush-on sealant is water-based, like Mod Podge products, but more permanent. I like its fast-drying qualities and smooth finish.*

E6000 Craft Adhesive: *The E6000 glue is my go-to when it comes to jewelry-making. It's great for sticking not-so-easy-to-stick surfaces together—like metal to metal, or anything to metal.*

PROJECT CONTRIBUTORS

In addition to my own projects, I called on some of my favorite crafters to re-create some of their most popular projects. If you'd like to see more of their work, check out their beautiful websites!

Allison Murray *dreamalittlebigger.com*
Personalized Coffee Tumbler, *page 41*

ChiWei Ranck *Idogwoof.com*
Custom Clipboard, *page 43*

Jenna Berger *jennaberger.com*
Wrapped Papier-Mâché Letters, *page 53*

Katie Waltemeyer *sweetrosestudio.com*
Shipshape Wall Art, *page 77*

Kathy Beymer *merrimentdesign.com*
Cross-Stitch Canvas, *page 81*

Susan Yates *crafterhoursblog.com*
Tumbling Gems Table Runner, *page 93*

In addition to the talented contributors, there are crafters whose work inspired me to include variations of their projects in these pages. They are:

Jamielyn Nye *iheartnaptime.net*
Doodle Dry-Erase Board, *page 143*

Natalie Pirveysian *cremedelacraft.com*
DIY Envelope Clutch, *page 157*

Melissa Klinker *mamamiss.com*
Popsicle Stick Bracelets, *page 179*

Marisa Edghill *omiyageblogs.ca*
Party Mask, *page 215*

Eighteen25 *eighteen25.blogspot.com*
Crafty Stick Frame, *page 293*

MEASUREMENT CONVERSION CHART

Imperial	Metric
⅛ inch	3.2 mm
¼ inch	6.4 mm
⅜ inch	10 mm
½ inch	13 mm
⅝ inch	1.6 cm
¾ inch	2 cm
1 inch	2.5 cm
4½ inches	11.4 cm
9 inches	23 cm
12 inches (1 foot)	30 cm
13½ inches	34.3 cm
18 inches	46 cm
22½ inches	57.2 cm
24 inches (2 feet)	61 cm
27 inches	68.6 cm
31½ inches	80 cm
36 inches (3 feet)	91 cm
39 inches	99 cm

ACKNOWLEDGMENTS

I always thank my mom first because she is the one who sent me to art classes and then to sewing camp when I was ten, even though I didn't want to go. Because of her I developed a lifelong love of crafting.

Thanks to my boyfriend, Steve, who has supported me through the highs and lows of life and learning how to run my own business. Thanks to my dogs, Roxie and Yoshi—they might not speak human language, but they are supportive roommates and coworkers.

Thanks to my friend and fellow enthusiast Maya, who is my partner in craftiness. Thanks to my contributors, Allison, Amber, Beverly, Cathe, Chi Wei, Heidi, Jenna, Johnnie, Kari, Kathy, Katie, Kim, Lidy, Morena, Pauline, Sarah, Susan, and Vanessa, who made beautiful projects for this book and are just awesome in general. Thanks to my agent, Katherine Latshaw, and my editor, Megan Nicolay, for being supportive and understanding when life had other plans for me during this book process. Thanks to Sarah Smith, who designed this impressive-looking book. Thanks to my business partner and friend Heather Mann, who has been with me on this magic blogging carpet ride since the beginning. Thank you to my amazing clients (you know who you are) because I couldn't do it without you.

And finally, thanks to my readers, who make my freelance life and ability to write books like this one possible—I try to make you proud on a daily basis! You'll never know how much I appreciate you.

ABOUT THE AUTHOR

AMY ANDERSON is a freelance writer, craft designer, and blogging entrepreneur. Her work has been featured in Huffington Post, *Better Homes & Gardens*, *Woman's Day*, *Wired*, and Design*Sponge, among others. Amy currently runs three successful craft blogs with more than 1 million combined monthly page views. She lives in Atlanta with her two furry dog friends and her boyfriend. You can typically find her crafting, wearing the color blue, drinking coffee, and contemplating what blogging venture to start next.